D0208036

The Secret Diary
of Adrian Mole Aged 13¾:
The Play

Sue Townsend's play, based on her internationally best-selling book, was created for the Phoenix Arts, Leicester, where it received its first production in September 1984. It was subsequently staged at Wyndham's Theatre, London, in December 1984.

This volume contains the complete text of the play with introductory notes on the staging by the author; the complete words of all the lyrics; and music for the melody line of each of the tunes.

Front cover design by Caroline Holden

Also by Sue Townsend

Fiction

The Secret Diary of Adrian Mole
    Aged 13¾

The Growing Pains of Adrian Mole

Plays

Bazaar and Rummage,
    Groping for Words
    & Womberang

The Great Celestial Cow

The Secret Diary
of Adrian Mole Aged 13¾

The Play

SUE TOWNSEND

with songs by KEN HOWARD and
ALAN BLAIKLEY

Methuen · London

A METHUEN PAPERBACK

First published in Great Britain as a Methuen Paperback
original in 1985
by Methuen London Ltd, 11 New Fetter Lane, London
EC4P 4EE
Reprinted 1986
Play copyright © 1985 by Sue Townsend
Music and lyrics copyright © 1985
by Ken Howard and Alan Blaikley, Axle Music Ltd.

Set in 9pt IBM Press Roman
by Words & Pictures Ltd, Thornton Heath, Surrey
and printed in Great Britain

British Library Cataloguing in Publication Data

Townsend, Sue
  The secret diary of Adrian Mole aged 13¾: the
  play.
  I. Title   II. Howard, Ken   III. Blaikley, Alan
  822'.914   PR6070.089/

  ISBN 0-413-59250-2

CAUTION
*Publication of this script does not necessarily indicate the
availability of performing rights in the play.*

*All amateur rights are controlled by Messrs. Samuel French,
52 Fitzroy Street, London W1P 6JR, to whom all such
enquiries should be made.*

*All other enquiries should be addresses to the author's agents,
Anthony Sheil Associates Ltd, 43 Doughty Street, London
WC1N 2LF.
Telephone 01-405 9351.*

*This paperback is sold subject to the condition that it shall
not, by way of trade or otherwise, be lent, resold, hired out,
or otherwise circulated without the publisher's prior consent
in any form of binding or cover other than that in which it is
published and without a similar condition including this
condition being imposed on the subsequent purchaser.*

Author's Note

If you are thinking of staging this play I send my very best wishes to you. I think it's quite a tricky play to stage. It is episodic and therefore flits about from scene to scene, and it demands a great deal from the young man who is to play Adrian Mole; a lot of lines to learn and moves to remember.

Graham Watkins, the director, and I were lucky in finding a superb young actor, Simon Schatzberger, to play the first Adrian Mole.

The play is set in Leicester and I think works best with East Midlands or Northern accents.

The Mole family are upwardly-mobile working-class; that is, they don't keep ferrets in the bath, and George Mole has bought his own house. The play had its first performance at the Phoenix Arts Centre in Leicester and translated very well (complete with Leicester accents) to the West End stage at Wyndham's Theatre.

Staging

The original production had an inspired setting. Anthony Dean designed a huge cut out dolls' house with a kitchen, hall and stairs, and living room downstairs; and a bathroom, Adrian's bedroom and his parents' bedroom upstairs. Gauzes and lighting effects were used to focus on specific rooms. Other scenes were played out in front of the house with the minimum of sets and furniture.

The play could work equally well with the simplest sets possible, or even none at all.

The Dog

The Mole dog is an important character. In the first production three puppets were used. A sitting-up dog, a lying-down, floppy dog and a show-stopping walking dog on wheels. The three puppets became unnaturally life-like in Simon's hands. However, if three puppets are beyond your budget, then try for at least one. If that's impossible, then go to the RSPCA and start training a real dog.

Voice-overs

Adrian's diary extracts are often used to link scenes, and should be pre-recorded. This gives the young actor a chance to breathe and reminds us that what we are seeing on stage has just been, or is about to be, written into a 'Secret Diary'.

Music
Ken Howard and Alan Blaikley have written some lovely songs. In Leicester the musical accompaniment was kept to the Scrooge-like minimum of two electric pianos and drums. In the West End it blossomed out into two electric pianos, drums and guitar. But should Joe Loss be your brother-in-law, then by all means ask him to play for you and arrange the band parts.

Style
The actors shouldn't have to break their necks for laughs — providing they go for the truth of what they are saying. Audiences are not thick and are capable of recognising and even laughing at a joke without having it pushed down their throats. Go for a good pace and try not to let it flag. And whether you are performing in the play or reading it at home, I hope you enjoy it.

Very Best Wishes,

Sue Townsend

The Secret Diary of Adrian Mole Aged 13¾ was first presented by
the Phoenix Theatre Company at the Phoenix Arts Centre,
Leicester, on 6 September 1984, with the following cast:

ADRIAN MOLE	Simon Schatzberger
GEORGE MOLE	Nigel Bennett
GRANDMA } QUEENIE	Betty Turner
MRS LUCAS MATRON DOREEN SLATER WOMAN ON TRAIN	Katy Feeney
PAULINE MOLE	Sheila Steafel
BERT BAXTER	David Davenport
MR LUCAS MR SCRUTON RICK LEMON	David Hobbs
PANDORA	Sara McGlasson
NIGEL BARRY KENT MR SINGH ELECTRICITY BOARD OFFICIAL	Antony Howes

Directed by Graham Watkins
Assistant Director Adrian Bean
Musical arrangements and direction by Mark Warman
Designed by Anthony Dean
Choreographed by Clive Hill
Lighting designed by Mike Seignior
Sound designed by Simon Galton

Musicians: Margaret Gundara (*synthesiser*)
Andrew Huggett (*drums*)
Mark Warman (*piano and synthesiser*)

This production subsequently opened at Wyndham's Theatre, London on 12 December 1984, with the following cast:

ADRIAN MOLE	Simon Schatzberger
PAULINE MOLE	Mandy Travis
GEORGE MOLE	Nigel Bennett
MR LUCAS	David Riley
MRS LUCAS	Katy Feeney
GRANDMA	Sheila Collings
NIGEL BARRY KENT ELECTRICITY MAN	Antony Howes
PANDORA	Katharine Schlesinger
SCHOOLGIRL	Louise Catt
KIDS IN DISCO	Michael Arch, Louise Catt, Ricky Simmonds
BERT BAXTER	David Davenport
DOREEN SLATER	Su Elliott
MR SCRUTON	Peter Richards
QUEENIE	Eileen Bell
MATRON	Sandra Fox

Directed by Graham Watkins
Musical staging by Christine Cartwright
Designed by Anthony Dean
Lighting by Mick Hughes
Sound by John Reddie
Musical arrangements and direction by Mark Warman

Musicians: Mark Warman (*piano and synthesiser*)
Charles Hart (*synthesisers*)
Fish (*guitars*)
Andrew Huggett (*drums*)

ACT ONE

Music: The Mole Overture.
At the end of the Overture, ADRIAN *comes to the front of the*
stage. He talks directly to the audience.

ADRIAN: This is just my luck! I've come all the way from
Leicester to hear a lecture about George Eliot only to be
thwarted at the last minute because the American lecturer
missed Concorde. What am I going to do now? I'm doing
George Eliot for my English Literature project. I've written
him loads of letters, but he hasn't replied to one. Still, with a
bit of luck I might be able to mingle with a few intellectuals
in the foyer. (*Looking round at the audience.*)
There's loads here tonight. But I bet *they* don't live an
ordinary life like me. No, they're lucky, they go home to
book-lined studies and intellectual families.
Perhaps when my diary is discovered people will understand
the torment of being a thirteen and three quarter-year old
intellectual. Until then I'll just have to put up with the
charade that is my family life.
I bet Malcolm Muggeridge's family didn't carry on like mine
did on New Year's Eve.

The lights go up to show the New Year's Eve party.
GRANDMA *and* MRS LUCAS *are sitting on the sofa.*
PAULINE *and* MR LUCAS *are dancing together.*
GEORGE *is drinking from a can of lager.*
ADRIAN *joins* NIGEL *at centre stage.*
Everyone, including ADRIAN *is wearing a party hat.*

NIGEL: I shall be glad to get home, I've been bored out of me
skull all night.

ADRIAN: I warned you not to come, Nigel. You should have
stayed at home with Andy Stewart . . . Do you want your
coat?

NIGEL: Yeah, I want to split, man.

ADRIAN: Why are you talking like an American?

NIGEL: Because I'm fed up with being English. I'm searching
for a new identity.

ADRIAN: You're never satisfied, Nigel.

NIGEL: So was that all you got for Christmas, a digital radio
alarm clock?

ADRIAN: Yes, that and the new *Beano* annual.

NIGEL: What's it like this year?

Adrian: It's a bit too childish now, for my taste.
> *Suggestive dancing from* MR LUCAS *and* PAULINE.
> *They go into the kitchen still dancing.* GRANDMA *watches disapprovingly.*

NIGEL: Is your mum drunk or does she always dance like that?

ADRIAN: She's drunk, I'm afraid.

NIGEL: It's embarassing watching adults trying to dance isn't it?

ADRIAN: It's enough to make you sick.

GRANDMA (*standing*): George! Coat!
> GEORGE *fetches* GRANDMA's *coat and helps her on with it.*

GRANDMA (*to* MRS LUCAS): It was very nice of you to talk to me. I enjoyed our chat about double glazing. Goodnight.

MRS LUCAS: Goodnight.
> MRS LUCAS *starts tidying up.*

GRANDMA: I shan't bother saying goodnight to Pauline. (*Raising her voice.*) I know she didn't want me at the party. Night, Adrian!

ADRIAN: Night, Grandma!
> GEORGE *and* GRANDMA *go off.*
> *In the kitchen* MR LUCAS *has his hands on* PAULINE's *shoulders, talking straight to her face. He is saying how long he has fancied her.*

NIGEL: You haven't seen my new bike yet, have you?

ADRIAN: No.

NIGEL: It was made by a craftsman in Nottingham.

ADRIAN: Mine was made by my dad in our back yard.

NIGEL: Honestly, Adrian, your consumer durables are a disgrace. Where's your mum?

MRS LUCAS: She's in the kitchen, I shouldn't go in. I think she's busy.

NIGEL: Right. (*Shouting.*) Thank you for the party, Mrs Mole. I shall remember it for the rest of my iife!

PAULINE (*in the kitchen*): 'Night, Nigel pet!
> PAULINE *and* MR LUCAS *separate.*

NIGEL: You can come round tomorrow and have a go on my Steve Davis snooker table if you like.

ADRIAN: I'm half way through a poem. I'm hoping to finish it tomorrow.

NIGEL: Suit yourself, Moley. 'Night Mrs Lucas. (*He leaves.*)

MRS LUCAS: 'Night, Nigel. Take care walking home. Don't get yourself mugged. (*Pause. She looks at* ADRIAN.) You look tired, love, why don't you go to bed?

ADRIAN: I've got to take the dog for a walk first. It's no wonder I'm short for my age.
ADRIAN *takes the walking dog out from under the stairs cupboard and goes off as* MR LUCAS *comes out of the kitchen.*

MR LUCAS (*to* MRS LUCAS): Right, you ready?

MRS LUCAS: Have you said 'Goodnight' to Pauline?

MR LUCAS: Yes, yes, come on. I want my bed.

MRS LUCAS: No you don't. You want Pauline's bed.

MR LUCAS: What's brought this on?

MRS LUCAS: I'm not blind, deaf and dumb. You're going to have an affair with her, aren't you?

MR LUCAS: I hardly know the woman.

MRS LUCAS: Well, who *are* you going to have an affair with then? You didn't buy yourself three pairs of Pierre Cardin underpants for nothing!

MR LUCAS: Look you agreed that we'd have an open marriage didn't you?

MRS LUCAS: Yes — open. But not *wide* open. Not the woman next door.

MR LUCAS: So it's a matter of geography now, is it?

MRS LUCAS: Look, I know that you need other women. It's a sort of hobby with you, isn't it? Like other men go potholing or sky-diving. But *they* don't do it in their own backyards, do they?

MR LUCAS: She's wasted on George. My God, he must be the most boring man in Leicester.

MRS LUCAS: Well, I'm going home to get some sleep. I'm knocking the kitchen wall down tomorrow. (*She starts to leave.*)

MR LUCAS (*raising his voice*): Look, I'm sorry. It's not my fault I was allocated too many hormones is it?

MRS LUCAS: There's no need to shout!

MR LUCAS: There's every need. We've got another bloody year to get through.
They go off.
PAULINE *comes out of the kitchen singing 'My Way'. She doesn't know the words.* GEORGE *comes in and watches her for a moment.*

GEORGE: Come on, duck, time for bed.

PAULINE: George I've got to tell you. It's my New Year's Resolution. (*Pause*.) George, nobody wears flared trousers nowadays. (*Pause*.) Nobody.

GEORGE (*looking at his flares*): Jim Reeves does.

PAULINE: But Jim Reeves is dead, George.

GEORGE: Jim Reeves will never die.

> *They go upstairs singing.* GEORGE *sings 'Your Hair of Gold'*
> PAULINE *sings 'My Way'.*
> ADRIAN *comes in, carrying the dog. It still has the lead around its neck.*

ADRIAN: The stupid thing only got the the end of the road before it collapsed. I've a good mind to report my father to the RSPCA. He shouldn't have made the dog drink all that cherry brandy at the party last night. (*He goes to the foot of the stairs and listens to* PAULINE *and* GEORGE *singing and arguing in the bedroom.*) There is a chance that my parents could be alcoholics. This time next year, I could be in a children's home. (*To the dog:*) You'd better sleep with me tonight.

> ADRIAN *goes upstairs with the dog. The lights go on in his bedroom. He puts the dog on the bed, and writes in his diary.*

ADRIAN (*voice over*): Just my luck. It's the first day of the New Year and I've got a spot on my chin where everyone can see it. It's my mother's fault for not knowing about vitamins.

> *The lights go down in the bedrooms.*

The lights are on in the living-room. GEORGE MOLE *is sitting in the untidy living-room fixing his model of the 'Marie Celeste.'* PAULINE *enters looking rough.*

PAULINE: George, I'm dying. (*She flops into a chair.*)

GEORGE: You deserve to be, Pauline. You drank enough Pernod to demolish the Thames Barrier

PAULINE: Well it's only once a year.

GEORGE: And I don't like the way you were dancing either.

PAULINE: I know I'm a bit out of practice but I didn't think I was that bad.

GEORGE: You were dancing in a suggestive, not to say wanton, manner. Mr Lucas got all of a doodah, I was watching him.

PAULINE: We were doing the *tango* George, we weren't Morris dancing. (PAULINE *gets up and starts to tidy up.*) Is Adrian up?

Lights go up in ADRIAN's *room to show* ADRIAN *trying to force an asprin down the dog's throat.*

GEORGE: He's trying to give the dog an asprin.

PAULINE: Why, what's up with it?

GEORGE: It's got a hangover.
ADRIAN *enters.*

PAULINE: You were the life and soul of the party again, weren't you Adrian? How many times have I told you? If you're not enjoying yourself, then *pretend* that you are. *I* have to do it at your lousy school concerts.

GEORGE: Have you been at my glue?

ADRIAN: No.

GEORGE: Well, it's not where I left it. You're sure you didn't take it up to your room for a quick snort?

PAULINE: As if he would.

GEORGE: That's what Jack at work said about his lad. Next thing Jack knows, his lad's been arrested for high-jacking a Bostik lorry. That's teenagers for you.

PAULINE: But Adrian's not a normal teenager, George.

ADRIAN: Yes I am!

PAULINE: Don't be silly, of course you're not. You're polite to me and your dad, you keep your room tidy and you don't play your stereo system at full decibels.

ADRIAN: I haven't got a stereo system, that's why!

GEORGE: We're not made of money, Adrian.

ADRIAN: I wasn't asking for one.

PAULINE: What's that on your chin?

ADRIAN: A spot.

PAULINE (*shuddering*): Uuugggh!

ADRIAN: It's because I don't get enough Vitamin C.

PAULINE: Go and buy an orange then.

GEORGE: Nobody talk to me. I'm rigging the sails.

PAULINE: Did you make any New Year's resolutions, petal?

GEORGE (*shouting*): I said don't talk to me!

PAULINE (*shouting*): I'm talking to Adrian!

ADRIAN: Yes, I made ten.

PAULINE: Oh, what were they?

ADRIAN: Oh, you know, helping the poor, stuff like that.

GEORGE: I'm glad to hear it. You can help me by turning your bedroom light off a bit earlier. And you left your heated rollers on again, Pauline.

PAULINE: You're getting obsessive about us using electricity.
You know that, don't you? You begrudge us every therm we
consume.
ADRIAN *goes out and sits on the stairs. He listens carefully to
the conversation.*

GEORGE (*gradually exploding*): Electricity is money, Pauline!
Hard earned money! And until you and him start bringing
some money into this house, I shall be as obsessive as I like. I
shall stand and watch the little wheel go round, I shall build a
bloody shrine around the meter cupboard, I shall . . .

PAULINE (*standing up*): Right that does it! I'm getting a job!

GEORGE (*standing up*): No wife of mine goes to work!

PAULINE: How many wives have you got?

GEORGE: Why can't you be happy to stay at home? You've got
it made. A little light housework in the morning. A quiet stroll
around the shops in the afternoon. Bit of telly in the evening.

PAULINE: You have just described a day in the life of a
convalescent snail! You sexist pig!

GEORGE: Here we go, here we go. She's read two chapters of
*The Female-*bloody-*Eunuch* and she's already surburbia's
answer to Greasy Greer.

PAULINE: It's Germaine.

GEORGE: Germane to what?

PAULINE: Let's not row, George. Not on the first day of the
New Year. Adrian will hear.

GEORGE (*bitterly*): Adrian, it's always Adrian! He's a
disappointment to me, Pauline, I don't mind admitting.

PAULINE: Just think, fourteen years ago he wasn't even here.

GEORGE: And then when he was here you wanted to send him
back.

PAULINE: Yes. He was an ugly baby though, wasn't he? . . . I
mean I know he's our son but . . .

GEORGE: Grotesque's the word. I've seen better looking
gargoyles.
GEORGE *and* PAULINE *laugh.* ADRIAN *is upset and angry.
He puts his raincoat on.*

PAULINE: I used to dread people looking into his pram. I had to
keep the cat net up permanently.
ADRIAN *comes forward.*
*The music to 'The House Where I Live' underplays the
following dialogue.*

ADRIAN: Bye!

PAULINE: Where are you going?

ADRIAN: Out. To buy an orange.
  GEORGE *and* PAULINE *go upstairs.*

The House Where I Live

ADRIAN (*sings*): She doesn't cook me my meals,
  Doesn't know how it feels
  To be hungry and young:
  And he doesn't budge from his chair,
  Doesn't care if I'm here – or there!

  Yes, this is my family seat,
  Eighteen Every Street –
  It's the house where I live.

  They ought to care if I smoke,
  Ask if I'm sniffing coke,
  Disapprove of my friends:
  I could be in some gangster's pay
  Or be wasting away, day by day!

  While they sit there sunk in their gloom
  I could meet with my doom
  In the house where I live.

  No cheerful fire in our hearth,
  Badedas in our bath,
  Aerosol in the loo:
  Who sees if we've run out of tea?
  Or the dog's done a pee? – It's me!

  Yes, here in its bleak monochrome
  Is my own broken home,
  It's the house where I live,
  Yes, this is my own broken home,
  It's the house where I live.

During the song, GEORGE *and* PAULINE *are seen in the house in separate rooms. By the end of the song, they are in bed together, in their bedroom. At the end of the song,* ADRIAN *takes off his coat and puts a lurex apron on.*

My parents have got the flu. This is just my luck! It was cough! cough! cough! last night. If it wasn't one, it was the other. You'd think they'd show some consideration. I've been up and down the stairs day and night with trays of food and drink.

MR *and* MRS LUCAS *enter. MR LUCAS is carrying a bouquet of flowers.*

MR LUCAS: Ah, young Adrian. As you see I bear a floral gift for the invalid.

MRS LUCAS: He means he's brought your mother some flowers (*Pause.*) Are you all right?

ADRIAN: No, I'm a bit worn out to tell you the truth and another worry is that the dog's left home.

MR LUCAS: Surely that's a cause for celebration?

MRS LUCAS: Bimbo!

ADRIAN: Oh I know it shouldn't have jumped on my father's model ship and got tangled up in the rigging, but there was no need for my father to threaten to have it put down. (*Pause.*) Shall *I* give her the flowers or do you want to see her?

MRS LUCAS: He wants to see her.

MR LUCAS (*going towards the stairs*): You go for Lurex in a big way do you, Adrian? . . . (*He laughs.*)

ADRIAN: I bought it for my mother for Christmas, but I haven't seen her wear it yet. (*He takes the apron off.*) My mother told me to warn her if any visitors came . . . to give her time to put her make-up on.

ADRIAN *goes upstairs to his parents' bedroom.*

MR LUCAS (*to* MRS LUCAS): Why are you still tagging on? Haven't you got a drain to clean or something?
(*They sit down to wait. Pause.*)

MRS LUCAS (*casually*): I was lying in bed last night trying to work out ways to kill you.

MR LUCAS: I thought you were reading.

MRS LUCAS: No. (*Pause.*) I decided on a seaside mishap.

MR LUCAS: Go on.

MRS LUCAS (*eagerly*): You know how you make me bury you up to your neck in cool sand when we're on the beach?

MR LUCAS: Yes.

MRS LUCAS: Well, I thought I'd just carry on and bury your ugly head as well. (*She smiles.*)

MR LUCAS: Very nice.

MRS LUCAS: I'd bring your body back to England, you wouldn't like to be buried in Benidorm, would you?

MR LUCAS (*shocked*): No.

MRS LUCAS: But then I decided against it.

MR LUCAS: I'm very pleased to hear it.

MRS LUCAS: No. I can't wait for the summer. Why don't we have a winter holiday instead? We could go skiing and I could chuck you over a precipice.

MR LUCAS: Wouldn't it be simpler to get a divorce?

MRS LUCAS: Oh it would be *simpler* but not half as satisfying. Look, can't you find yourself a young, single girl? The wine bars are full of them.

MR LUCAS: I want Pauline.

MRS LUCAS: And Adrian. He's part of the package.

MR LUCAS: I don't mind. I've always wanted a son and Adrian's past the stage of screaming in the night.

MRS LUCAS: If we'd had children it wouldn't have made any difference. We've got nothing in common. (*As she goes off.*) I'm a woman and you're a man!
MR LUCAS prepares himself to see PAULINE. *He combs his hair and sprays breath freshener into his mouth.*
The lights go up in PAULINE's *bedroom to show* PAULINE *sitting up in bed applying lipstick.* GEORGE *is also in the bed.* ADRIAN *is standing next to the bed.*

ADRIAN: Shall I tell him you're ready?

PAULINE (*spraying perfume onto herself and into the air*): Just a minute. I must get rid of the smell of the sick-room.

GEORGE: You can tell him I'm asleep.
GEORGE *pulls the sheet over his head.*

ADRIAN (*shouting downstairs*): She's ready!

GEORGE: What's *he* coming round for? I didn't visit him when he had haemorroids, did I? I left him in peace.

PAULINE: He's only being neighbourly, George. Put the sheet back over your head.
MR LUCAS walks upstairs. GEORGE *reads the* Daily Express *under the sheets.* MR LUCAS *enters the bedroom.* MR LUCAS *and* PAULINE *stare* ADRIAN *out.*
ADRIAN goes to his room to write his diary. MR LUCAS *sits on* PAULINE's *side of the bed. He hands her the flowers. He kisses his fingers and transfers the kiss to* PAULINE's *lips.*
PAULINE is conscious of GEORGE *awake under the sheets.*

Mr Lucas, how kind of you! They're beautifully unnatural! They must have cost a fortune! ·

MR LUCAS: No sweat, Mrs Mole. I know a bloke at Interflora.

PAULINE: George will love them when he wakes up.

MR LUCAS: Been asleep long, has he?

PAULINE: No, he's just dropped off.
PAULINE *says 'He's awake' in dumb show.*

MR LUCAS: I won't stay long, I just wanted to see you . . . (*He takes* PAULINE's *hand and presses it to his mouth, almost eats it.*) . . . and George.

PAULINE: Well, I'll tell George you came. He'll be sorry to have missed you.
(*She grabs* MR LUCAS's *hand and kisses it.*) How's Mrs Lucas?

MR LUCAS: She's well, she sends her love.
MR LUCAS *kisses* PAULINE's *neck and shoulders.* PAULINE *tries to wrench his head away. During the following dialogue,* MR LUCAS *and* PAULINE *kiss, cuddle, touch etc.*

PAULINE: I do admire your wife, the way she installed your gas central heating single-handed! I'm so helpless myself. I have to get George to change the light bulbs.

MR LUCAS: You're a very feminine woman, Mrs Mole. You don't want to be messing about with light bulbs. I'm sure you've got other skills at your fingertips. Artistic skills . . .

PAULINE: Oh I have, I have, but I haven't used them for so long . . .
GEORGE *turns over in bed.* MR LUCAS *and* PAULINE *fly apart.* MR LUCAS *picks up* The Female Eunuch.

MR LUCAS: Bedside reading eh? (*He reads.*) *The Female Eunuch.* Yes I've heard of that. I read a book once . . .

PAULINE: Did you? What was it called?

MR LUCAS: It was called *I Want You.*

PAULINE (*frantically*): I don't think I'm familiar with that title. *The Female Eunuch* is *very good*; it's making me re-think a lot about my role as a woman. Fixing my own light bulbs for instance.
GEORGE *grunts.*

PAULINE: He's talking in his sleep.

MR LUCAS: Well, there'll be murder done if I don't get home to the wife. So, I'll love you and leave you, Mrs Mole. Any idea when you'll be back in circulation?

PAULINE: It will be very, very soon.
    They blow each other kisses. MR LUCAS *goes.*
GEORGE: I've never heard such a load of silly slobber in the
    whole of my life.
PAULINE: Oh stuff some Vick up your nose and shut up!

ADRIAN *comes downstairs wearing his school uniform and
carrying his briefcase. He comes downstage. The lights go up on a
school wall and netball post.*
ADRIAN: When Mr Lucas went, my father had an argument with
    my mother and made her cry. My father is still in a bad mood.
    This means he is feeling better. I made my mother a cup of tea
    without her asking, this made her cry as well. You just can't
    please some people!
    PANDORA *enters bouncing a netball. She practices shooting
    at the net.*
    There is a new girl at our school. Her name is Pandora but she
    likes to be called 'Box'. Don't ask me why. I might fall in love
    with her. It's time I fell in love. After all, I am thirteen and
    three quarters years old.
    ADRIAN *stands staring at* PANDORA.
PANDORA: Do you mind? You're ruining my concentration.
ADRIAN: Sorry. I was just admiring the way you handled the
    ball.
PANDORA: Netball is a ridiculous game. So one gets the stupid
    ball in the stupid net. Who cares?
ADRIAN: Well you're very good at it.
PANDORA: I'm good at most things.
ADRIAN: I'm no good at sport.
PANDORA: How boring for you.
ADRIAN: Oh, I don't mind. I'm more the intellectual sort.
    PANDORA *turns to look at* ADRIAN.
PANDORA: Are you clever as well as being intellectual?
ADRIAN: No. I'm about average really.
PANDORA: You poor thing. What *do* you excel in?
ADRIAN: I write poetry.
PANDORA: Juvenile stuff I suppose.
ADRIAN: Well I *am* a juvenile.
PANDORA: Boring isn't it? Hanging around waiting to grow up.
    I mean what's the point? One's no longer a child, so why go
    through this dreary half and half stage?

ADRIAN: You used to go to a posh school didn't you?

PANDORA: Yes, but then Mummy and Daddy got a conscience about it. They're both socialists, so they threw me into the comprehensive system.

ADRIAN: Do you like it?

PANDORA: One school is very much like another, isn't it? All that shouting and bullying. Teachers are the same everywhere. Fascists.

ADRIAN: What, like Hitler, you mean?

PANDORA: Oh yes. Well, perhaps not *quite* as bad as him. But they do rather think that they're the master race, don't they?

ADRIAN: You go to the 'Off the Streets' Youth Club, don't you?

PANDORA: Yes, there's rather a banal disco on tonight, isn't there?

ADRIAN *stares.*

What are you staring at?

ADRIAN: Your eyes. They're the same colour as our dog's.

PANDORA: What sort of dog is it?

ADRIAN: It's a mongrel.

PANDORA: Gee thanks!

NIGEL *enters wearing whatever is current teenage high fashion.*

NIGEL: Hi, Box!

PANDORA (*pleased*): Oh hello, Nigel. You look brillo pad.

NIGEL: Thanks.

ADRIAN: Where's your uniform?

NIGEL: In the cloakroom. I'm going to town to buy some gear to wear to the disco tonight.

ADRIAN: Why can't you wear your uniform in town?

NIGEL: I'd sooner die.

PANDORA (*to* ADRIAN): Somebody might see him.

NIGEL (*to* PANDORA): Are you having a relationship at the moment?

PANDORA: No, actually I'm just recovering from one.

NIGEL: Like me. I've just broken one off. She was three-timing me.

PANDORA: Still it gives one the chance to draw breath doesn't it? Have a look round, see what's available.

NIGEL: Well, I'm available.

PANDORA: Well, we'll have to see what fate has in store for us, won't we?
She goes off watched by NIGEL *and* ADRIAN.

ADRIAN: Oh God, she's beautiful! She's got hair like treacle.

NIGEL: What, sticky?

ADRIAN: No! It's the colour of golden syrup.

NIGEL: You're in love with her, aren't you?

ADRIAN: Yes.

NIGEL *puts his arm round* ADRIAN.

NIGEL: Well forget it, Moley. You're not in the same division. She's a class bird. She won't *look* at a guy unless he's got at least a hundred quid's worth on his back and you've got to have the right brand names — the right labels.

ADRIAN: OK. If you're the expert on clothes tell me what intellectuals wear.

NIGEL: Why?

ADRIAN: Because I think I'm turning into one. It must be all the worry.

NIGEL: When did you turn?

ADRIAN: Last night. I saw Malcolm Muggeridge on the telly and I understood nearly every word.

NIGEL: Well, write to *him* and ask him what to wear.

ADRIAN: I don't know where he lives do I?

NIGEL: Well write to him care of the British Museum then, that's where all the intellectuals hang out isn't it? See you.
NIGEL *goes off.*

ADRIAN (*with contempt*): The British Museum! Intellectuals don't waste their time looking at old statues and stuff, they're too busy writing poems and appearing on BBC book programmes. Yes! I'll write to Mr Muggeridge care of the BBC. I'd better enclose a stamped addressed envelope because Mr Muggeridge *is* an old aged pensioner and probably can't afford a first class stamp. I'll soon be an expert on old aged pensioners. I've joined a group at school called The Good Samaritans. We go round doing good in the community and stuff. The old people were shared out at break today. I got an old man called Bert Baxter. He's eighty-nine so I don't suppose I'll have him for long.

At the youth club disco. Loud music. Dim lights. NIGEL *pogos onto the stage. He is dressed as a weekend punk. He dances for a while in a madly exhibitionist style. The music is turned down in volume.* NIGEL *reacts angrily.*

NIGEL: Hey! Where's the sounds?

ADRIAN *enters dressed in shirt, sweater, tie and school trousers.*

ADRIAN: That's better, it was hurting my ears. I asked Rick Lemon to turn it down.

NIGEL: Haven't you been to a disco before, Mole?

ADRIAN: No.

NIGEL: Thought not. You look like Frank Bough. Go and stand in the corner. I'm ashamed to be seen with you. Don't you care what you look like?

ADRIAN: No. I don't. (*Pause.*) You look dead stupid. Doesn't your mother mind you being a punk at weekends?

NIGEL: No. Not so long as I wear my string vest under my bondage tee-shirt.

ADRIAN: You're not a proper punk, are you? I thought proper punks had safety pins in their ears.

NIGEL: They do. I forgot to put mine in.

PANDORA *enters.*

PANDORA: Oh, it's Adrian Mole. In the half light I thought it was an old Crumblie.

ADRIAN: Crumblie?

PANDORA: Somebody over twenty-five.

ADRIAN: You look very nice from what I can see. Is it always dark at discos?

NIGEL (*to* PANDORA): It's his first time.

PANDORA (*laughs*): Incredible! Never been to a disco before?

ADRIAN: No. And I don't think I'll bother again.

NIGEL (*to* PANDORA): I came out without putting my safety pin in my ear. So I'm just about to do it now. You can watch if you like. *He takes a safety pin from his tee-shirt.*

PANDORA: Oh you are brave — stupid, but brave.

ADRIAN *watches, horrified, as* NIGEL *inserts the safety pin.* Well done!

NIGEL: Oh, it's killing me! Get it out!

ADRIAN: It's your own fault for showing off. (*He gives* NIGEL *a tissue.*)

NIGEL: I'm bleeding. Look — blood! It's pouring! I'm going to die!

PANDORA: It *is* gushing out, rather.

NIGEL: Take me to the hospital. Get an ambulance!
PANDORA comforts NIGEL *who is now close to fainting. They go off to loud disco music.* ADRIAN *comes to the front of the stage. He talks to the audience.*

ADRIAN: My father had to take Nigel to the hospital in our car. Nigel's parents haven't got a car because his father's got a steel plate in his head and isn't allowed to drive and his mother is only four feet eleven inches tall so she can't reach the pedals. It's not surprising Nigel has turned out bad really, with a maniac and a midget for parents.

ADRIAN: Today was the most terrible day of my life: I've got fifteen spots on my shoulders, my father is in a bad mood — he thinks his big-end is going, Pandora is going out with Nigel, but, worst of all, Bert Baxter is not a nice old age pensioner!
The lights go up to show BERT BAXTER *sitting half-undressed in a television chair. Empty beer bottles are under the chair, also an enormous jar of beetroot. A dog's bowl is beside the chair. An alsatian dog barks loudly offstage.*

BERT (*fiercely*): Who's there?
ADRIAN *is half in the door.*

ADRIAN (*desperately*): Can I come in, please? I think your dog's trying to bite me.

BERT: Bite yer! 'Ell 'ave yer bleddy leg off. He's a pure, thoroughbred, radged-up Alsation, ain't yer Sabre? (*Sabre answers with a bark.*) Quiet, sir! (*Sabre is instantly quiet.*) Who are you?

ADRIAN (*squeezes in*): I'm Adrian Mole from Neil Armstrong Comprehensive School.

BERT: You got me out of bed.

ADRIAN: Sorry, I thought you'd be up.

BERT: Why?

ADRIAN: It's the afternoon!

BERT: What's that got to do with ought? A man of my age needs his sleep. (*He sticks a Woodbine in his mouth.*) Got a light?

ADRIAN: No. I don't smoke.

BERT (*shocked*): Don't smoke! A lad of your age! You should be ashamed of yourself!
Sabre goes crazy behind the door.

(*Roaring*): Quiet, sir! (*To* ADRIAN:) He's hungry. You
wouldn't have a spare tin of dog food on you, would you?

ADRIAN: No. (*Pause.*) Mr Baxter, the school sent you a letter
about me. It was to warn you that I'd be coming round.

BERT: Why, what are you — a burglar?

ADRIAN: No. I'm a Good Samaritan. I go round doing good in
the community.

BERT: What for?

A long pause.

ADRIAN: I miss maths.

BERT: So you've come round here to do me some good, have
you?

ADRIAN: Yes, is ther anything you'd like me to do.

BERT: Yes, bugger off!

ADRIAN: Then could you sign my paper to prove that I've been?

BERT: No. I never sign nothin', that way they can't get you.

ADRIAN: Who?

BERT: The Government.

ADRIAN: But it's only for the school.

BERT: Schools is run by governments, ain't they? Don't you
know ought? (BERT *slaps his legs.*) Come on me old beauties!
Here, you can go and get me shoppin' in for me. Now
concentrate because I'm going to tell you what I want and I
'ate repeatin' myself. Twenty Woodies.

ADRIAN: Woodies?

BERT: Woodbines, lad. Concentrate. A jar of beetroot, a tin of
Chum, three bottles of brown ale and the *Morning Star*.

ADRIAN: Is the *Morning Star* a newspaper?

BERT: What's up wi' you, lad? Are you backward? The *Morning
Star* is the only newspaper worth readin'. The others are
owned by capitalist runnin' dog lackeys.

ADRIAN: So — Twenty Woodies. A jar of beetroot. A tin of
Chum. Three bottles of brown ale. The *Morning Star*. Could I
have the money, please?

BERT: Tell 'em to put it on my account. On account of how I've
got no money left.

BERT *laughs and goes off.*

Sinister music as BARRY KENT *enters.*

KENT: Mole! You weren't at school this morning, Mole.
He sprays 'B.K. OK?' on a wall. ADRIAN *tries to leave without being seen.* BARRY KENT *has his back turned.*

KENT: Stay where you are, Mole!
Where you bin, Mole — Skivin'?
ADRIAN *stands perfectly still with his back turned to* KENT.

ADRIAN: No. I've been out, being a Good Samaritan.
ADRIAN *starts to go off.*

KENT: I said, stay where you are.
KENT *puts the full stops on his graffiti.*

ADRIAN: I've got to go. I've got a test on the Norwegian Leather Industry . . .

KENT: Who gives a toss about the Norwegian Leather Industry?

ADRIAN: I do. I'm a bit of an expert. I expect to get full marks. Let me go.

KENT: I ain't touched you. You could go if you wanted to.

ADRIAN: You know I can't.
KENT *approaches* ADRIAN.

KENT: Give me twenty-five pence an' you can go freely on Her Majesty's footpaths.

ADRIAN: I haven't got twenty-five pence.

KENT: You got your dinner money, ain't you?

ADRIAN: I haven't. My dad pays by cheque since it went up to seventy pence a day.
KENT *straightens* ADRIANS's *tie.*

KENT: All you poofters have pocket money, don't you? For helping your mummies with the washing up?

ADRIAN: Mine goes straight into the Market Harborough Building Society. All I get is sixteen pence a day — for a Mars bar.

KENT: Oh dear, oh dear. Then you're in trouble, Mole 'cos I need twenty-five pence a day from you, so's I can maintain my present life-style. You seen the price of Doc Martens?
KENT *twists* ADRIAN's *arm.*

ADRIAN: You're hurting me, a bit.

KENT: Sorry, gotta do it. I ain't 'ad your advantages.
KENT *continues hurting* ADRIAN.

ADRIAN: Now you're hurting me a lot.

Sorry, Gotta Do It
During which KENT *beats* ADRIAN *up and kicks him in the goolies and generally humiliates him.*

KENT: Sorry, gotta do it, gotta do it,
    Sorry, gotta do it,
    Sorry, gotta do it, gotta do it, gotta do it:
    Nothing personal − know what I mean?

    What you need is my protection:
    In return I take collection
    Of a paltry pound or three − it
    Makes good sense! Invest in me! Like

    You're the client, I'm the banker:
    I need finance, you're a wanker!
    Things are as they ought to be, now
    I've got you and you've got me − see?

    Sorry, gotta do it, gotta do it,
    Sorry, gotta do it,
    Sorry, gotta do it, gotta do it, gotta do it:
    Nothing personal − know what I mean?

    Breathe a word and you'll regret it!
    Think of squealing? Don't forget, it's
    Me you'll have to answer to − and
    In the end, I *will* get you! I'll

    Have your little guts for garters,
    Mash your face in − just for starters!
    'Cause you know my golden rule is
    No holds barred! Go for the goolies!

    Sorry, gotta do it, gotta do it,
    Sorry, gotta do it,
    Sorry gotta do it, gotta do it, gotta do it:
    Nothing personal − know what I mean?

    The song ends with KENT *standing triumphantly over* ADRIAN *who is crying.*

ADRIAN: I've changed my mind. I will give you twenty-five pence a day after all. I'll get a paper round.

KENT: Well that's real decent of you, Mole. 'Ere have a tissue. I ain't heartless.
    He throws ADRIAN *a Kleenex and goes off.* ADRIAN *wipes his eyes, blows his nose, then stands and tidies himself up.*

ADRIAN: Woke up next day with a pain in my goolies.

ADRIAN *picks up a newspaper sack. He sees* PANDORA *crossing the stage wearing her riding hat and jodhpurs. He hides until she's gone. He looks at the papers he is to deliver to her house.*

ADRIAN (*to the audience*): Pandora lives at 69 Elm Tree Avenue. They have *The Guardian, Punch, Private Eye* and *New Society.* Pandora reads *Jackie* — the comic for girls; so she is not an intellectual like me. But I don't suppose Malcolm Muggeridge's wife is either.

ADRIAN *crosses to the house, reading* The Guardian. *He stops at the threshhold. He turns to the audience.*

It's full of spelling mistakes! It is disgusting when you think of how many people who can spell are out of work.

He goes upstairs to his bedroom and writes in his diary.

(*Voice over:*) Pandora has got a little fat horse called Blossom. She feeds it and makes it jump over barrels every morning before school. She looked dead good in her riding stuff. Her chest was wobbling like mad. She will need to wear a bra soon. *The lights are up on* ADRIAN's *bedroom, and* PAULINE *is in the bathroom cleaning the loo.*

(*To the audience:*) My mother came into my room this morning and started mumbling on about 'Adult relationships' and 'life being complicated' and how she must 'find herself'. She said she was fond of me. 'Fond'!!! and would hate to hurt me, and then she said that for some women marriage was like being in prison.

PAULINE *comes downstairs, puts her coat on.*

Marriage is nothing like being in prison. Women are let out every day to go to the shops and quite a few go to work. I think my mother is being a bit melodramatic.

PAULINE: Adrian, I'm off to my 'Women's Workshop on Assertiveness Training'. When your father comes home, tell him his dinner is in the freezer. (*Pause.*) At Sainsbury's. GEORGE MOLE *enters from work.*

GEORGE: I'm home! (*Pause.*) Pauline, I'm home! (*Silence.*) (*Mimicking* PAULINE:) Oh, hello George, how lovely to see you. How many storage heaters did you sell today? You sit down there in front of the telly, I'll bring your dinner in to you. (*In his own voice:*) What are we eating, Pauline? (*Mimicking* PAULINE:) Home-made steak and kidney pie, followed by spotted dick and custard! (*In his own voice:*) Yum, yum! Come here, wife.

ADRIAN *watches from the stairs.*

(*Mimicking* PAULINE:) Oh, George! Don't! The dinner will spoil! Oh, all right then . . .(*In his own voice, bitterly:*) Some bloody hope!

ADRIAN *enters.*
Where's your mother?

ADRIAN: Gone to a women's workshop on assertiveness training.
GEORGE *swears under his breath.*
What *is* assertiveness training?

GEORGE: God knows, but it sounds like bad news for me!

ADRIAN: She's bought herself some of those overalls that
painters and decorators wear.

GEORGE: Was she wearing her high heels with it?

ADRIAN: Yes.

GEORGE: So there's still hope. Lipstick?

ADRIAN: Yes, but it was that lip gloss stuff, not her usual
orange.

GEORGE: I knew it. Give her a fortnight and she'll be running
around in monkey boots and a bristly hair cut. They've no
right to interfere!

ADRIAN: Who?

GEORGE: Those bloody workshop types. They go around
stirring women up telling them they're unhappy. (*Small pause.*)
Is there a boil-in-the-bag cod-in-butter sauce left in the freezer?

ADRIAN: No, she hasn't been to Sainsbury's. She's been looking
after Mr Lucas.

GEORGE: What's up with him?

ADRIAN: Mrs Lucas is leaving him. They're getting a divorce.
Poor Mr Lucas is dead upset.

GEORGE: Poor Mr Lucas could *be* dead for all I care.

ADRIAN: You don't like him, do you?

GEORGE: No.

ADRIAN: Why? He's ever so nice and he really appreciates what
mum's doing for him.

GEORGE: What *is* she doing for him?

ADRIAN: She's comforting him for his tragic loss.
GEORGE *swears under his breath.*

GEORGE: Is there any bacon in the house?

ADRIAN: There's one slice.

GEORGE: Where?

ADRIAN: It's on the floor between the fridge and the cooker.
It's been there for *three days* to my knowledge!

GEORGE: It's bloody disgusting how she keeps this house lately,
my socks have been in the Ali Baba basket for over a week!

ADRIAN: I can't remember the last time she bothered to wash my PE kit. I have to do it myself or take it round to Grandma's.

GEORGE: Poor kid. I'm very fond of your mother, Adrian, very very fond. But she's beginning to be a bit of a handful. Perhaps it's hormone trouble . . . (*Flinging his shoes across the floor.*) Switch the telly on, kid.
Television noise. Lights down. The TV closedown tone is heard. They sleep. PAULINE enters. Lights up. She holds herself aggressively. Her voice is firm. She addresses GEORGE and ADRIAN who are still asleep. She is holding a large piece of card.

PAULINE (*loudly*): Right!
ADRIAN and GEORGE wake up.
The worm has turned! Things are going to be different around here! I am holding in my hand a chart; as you see, it is divided into three columns. Each column represents a member of this family. This is me, this is you, George, and this is Adrian.

ADRIAN: What's all that writing under my name?

PAULINE: It is a list of household jobs. The first job on your list, Adrian, reads 'clean lavatory'. I know you think a little gang of fairies come out at night and fly round with the Harpic, but you are wrong. A *person* cleans the lavatory and until now that person has been me. But not any more. (*She pins the chart up.*) We start tomorrow!

There is fast Mole music, then strobe light as ADRIAN runs around doing housework.

ADRIAN (*voice over*): Cleaned toilet, washed basin and bath before doing my paper round. Came home, made breakfast, put washing in machine, went to school. Gave Barry Kent his menaces money, went to Bert Baxter's, waited for social worker who didn't come, had school dinner. Had domestic science — made apple crumble. Came home. Vacuumed hall, lounge and breakfast room. Peeled potatoes, chopped up cabbage. Cut finger, rinsed blood off cabbage. Put chops under grill. Looked in cookery book for a recipe for gravy. Made gravy. Strained lumps out with a colander. Set table, served dinner, washed up. Put burnt saucepans in to soak. Got washing out of machine; everything blue, including white underwear and handkershiefs. Hung washing on clothes horse. Fed dog. Ironed PE kit. Cleaned shoes. Did homework. Took dog for a walk.
ADRIAN crosses the stage with the dog. He comes back on stage.

ADRIAN (*to the audience*): Just my luck to have an assertive mother!
Lights up on MR LUCAS *and* PAULINE *in the kitchen.*

MR LUCAS: Paulie, Paulie. What we've got is something very rare and precious. We're like two sunbeams dancing on the ceiling of life. Together we could make a new sun, a new planet. We're cosmic, Pauline!

PAULINE: Stop it! I can't think straight when you talk like that.

MR LUCAS: *I* can't think straight. I'm losing customers. I keep catching myself saying 'Oh why worry about the future?' It's not a healthy attitude for an insurance man to have. Don't think, Pauline. Just act. Come away with me!

PAULINE: I keep seeing the expression on Adrian's face the day his mouse died. He came home from junior school. I said: 'Hello pet, your mouse is dead.' He took it very badly.

MR LUCAS (*sulking*): Look, I'm not here to chat about dead pets. Pauline. (*He turns away.*)

PAULINE: Oh come on, love! Since you moved next door, I've had colour in my life; excitement. I couldn't wait to hang my washing out in the morning. 'Will he be in the garden?' I used to get through a Euro-sized packet of Ariel a week.

MR LUCAS: Did you? Did you really?

PAULINE: Yes, not to mention the Comfort.

MR LUCAS: I'll be your comfort, and your joy, and your support. Your bodily lover, your spiritual helpmate, your companion in old age. I'll be your true, true love. Tell him tonight, Pauline, or I'm going to Beachy Head.

PAULINE: Have you got relations there?

MR LUCAS: No, Paulie, pet. I shall chuck myself onto the rocks! I can't face life without my little sunbeam.
They are now just about to make love on the floor. ADRIAN *comes downstairs and tries to get into the kitchen.*

ADRIAN: Mum, are you in there?

PAULINE: Yes, me and Mr Lucas are . . . mending the boiler. Can't it wait? Only I've got my hands full.

ADRIAN: Have I got any clean socks? (*Shouts:*) Hello, Mr Lucas!

MR LUCAS (*shouts*): Hello, Adrian!

PAULINE: I forgot to take them out of the washer. Sorry, sunbeam.

ADRIAN: I'll wear yesterday's again then, (*To himself:*) Sunbeam?
There is a lighting change.

ADRIAN (*to the audience*): Went to school. Found it closed.
What with all the worry I had forgotten that I am on holiday.
I didn't want to go home, so I went to see Bert Baxter instead.
I asked him if he would like to see a horse again. He said he
would, so I took him to see Blossom. It took us ages to get
there. Bert walks dead slow and he kept having to sit down on
garden walls. Bert said that Blossom was not a horse, she was a
girl pony. He kept patting her and saying 'Who's a beauty
then, eh?'
Then we walked back to Bert's house. I went to the shops and
bought a packet of Vesta chow mein and a butterscotch
Instant Whip for our dinner, so Bert ate a decent meal for once.
We watched 'Pebble Mill at One', then Bert showed me his old
horse brushes.
Lights up on BERT *with horse brushes.* ADRIAN *crosses to him.*

BERT: I turned into a Communist before it became generally
popular. I were one of the first. It happened on August 11th,
1910. At 2 o'clock. As you know, I were an ostler. That's
doin' things with 'osses.
Well, one day, I'd got the 'osses brushed and gleamin'. It
were a 'ot day, so I'd got a bit of a muck sweat on myself,
when the lady of the house comes round the stables. She had
her friend with her, pretty little thing in a blue dress, wi' a lace
collar like a collection of snow flakes. Any road up, these
ladies are wrinkling their little noses up on account of the
smell of the 'oss shit.
The lady of the house says: 'I say Baxter, is there nothing you
can do about the smell in here?' I says: 'No Mum, not unless
you can stop the 'osses shitting!' Well, you should have heard
the carry on. You'd a' thought I'd said summat rude! I 'ad
tuppence docked out o' me wages. Then, later on that night, I
seen the lady of the house feedin' chocolate eclairs to one of
me best horses. Chocolate eclairs cost thruppence each — it
were then I turned into a Communist!

ADRIAN: Why didn't you join the Labour Party, Bert?

BERT: You know nought lad. Anyway, we were that poor, we
never 'ad one.

The Bad Old Days

BERT *sings to* ADRIAN. *At various points throughout the
song,* BERT *and* ADRIAN *march and dance.*

Bert (*sings*): When I was just your age, son,
When I was just a lad,
Things were far different then

I can tell you, my friend—
They were ten times as bad!
Had me no gilded youth, boy,
Lit by no sunshine rays —
We were fourteen in a hovel,
Takin' lessons how to grovel,
In the bad old days.

Lenin's my hero still, boy—
He was a man of steel:
If he came back today
His hair would turn grey
At the whole lousy deal!
Paid up and joined the Party,
Carried the big red flag:
We were comrades in an army,
Though they told us we were barmy,
In the bad old days.

They dance.

We toiled our youth away, boy —
No money, no thanks, no praise:
They say 'Where there's muck there's brass' —
I say "Not on your bloomin. arse!"
They were bad old days.
ADRIAN *and* BERT *go off.*

Lights go up on the LUCAS. *garden. A trough of flowers and a gnome decorate the space.* MRS LUCAS *is uprooting trees and putting them into a wheelbarrow. She is wearing wellingtons and overalls. It is twilight.*

PAULINE: Adrian said that you wanted to see me. (*Pause.*) Do you want any help with that bush?

MRS LUCAS: No thanks, I'm stronger than I look. (*Pause.*) I'm leaving Derek tonight. I thought you ought to know.

PAULINE: Who's Derek?

MRS LUCAS: That's your lover's name. He wasn't christened 'Bimbo'.

PAULINE: I can't think of him as being a Derek.

MRS LUCAS: Does he still talk about sunbeams?

PAULINE: They've been mentioned in passing.

MRS LUCAS: 'Two sunbeams dancing on the ceiling of life.' He knows how to get us going does Bimbo.

PAULINE: I love him.

MRS LUCAS: I know, I did once.

PAULINE: I'm ever so sorry. I like you a lot. Oh — put that tree down!

PAULINE *holds* MRS LUCAS*'s hand.*

MRS LUCAS: I've fallen for somebody myself. I may as well tell you. Make you feel better perhaps.

PAULINE: Oh, I'm so glad. What's his name?

MRS LUCAS: *Her* name is Glenys.

PAULINE *drops* MRS LUCAS*'s hand.*

PAULINE: Oh, I see.

MRS LUCAS: You're shocked, aren't you?

PAULINE: Well, I am a bit. You don't expect it in a cul-de-sac somehow.

PAULINE *grabs* MRS LUCAS*'s hand again.*

MRS LUCAS: You never know about people. There are things you don't know about him. Will you take Adrian with you?

PAULINE: I don't know. It's hard to uproot a kid, they're not like trees.

MRS LUCAS: But at least I'll see these grow. Goodnight. Good luck with Derek.

She pushes the wheelbarrow off stage. It has got dark.

PAULINE: Good luck with Glenys.

GEORGE *enters the garden, shining a torch.*

GEORGE: Pauline!

PAULINE: I'm here!

GEORGE: What are you doing standing in the dark?

PAULINE: I've been talking to Mrs. Lucas. About trees.

GEORGE: You're shivering. Come in, love. I've turned the thermostat up. It's lovely and warm at home. And I've got Jim Reeves on the turntable.

PAULINE: What's Adrian doing?

GEORGE: He's in his room. Why?

PAULINE: Do you think he'd miss me, if I died, or went away?

GEORGE: Have you been drinking, Pauline? Of course he'd bloody miss you. You're his mother. (*Pause.*) You haven't got any health problems you've not told me about, have you?

PAULINE: No.

GEORGE: What's all this silly slobber about dying and going away for then?

PAULINE: I'm just being daft, take no notice.

GEORGE: You've not been yourself lately.

PAULINE (*quickly*): George, I'm in love with another man.
A long pause.

GEORGE: You mean other than me?

PAULINE: Yes. I said *another* man.
A small pause.

GEORGE: What's his name?

PAULINE: Derek.

GEORGE: Thank god for that. It's usually someone you know. You'll have to give me a minute, Pauline. My body's stopped working. I can't move it.
GEORGE *is motionless.*

PAULINE: Derek is Bimbo, Mr Lucas. We're standing in his back garden.
GEORGE *gives a long anguished moan of despair and anger. He drops to his knees.*
Don't, love, don't. Oh, I'm so sorry. I wish it hadn't happened.
GEORGE *clasps* PAULINE's *legs.*

GEORGE: Don't leave me, Pauline.

PAULINE: I've got to. I can't live next door to the man I love!

GEORGE (*desperately*): I'll build you a car port then you can go and see him without getting wet.

PAULINE: We'll have to talk it over in a civilised manner, the three of us. We're all intelligent people, we can work something out. Tonight. (*She starts to go off.*)

GEORGE: Where are you going?

PAULINE: To tell Bimbo.

GEORGE: What about Adrian?

PAULINE (*crying*): I can't tell him. You'll have to. I told him about his mouse!
PAULINE *goes off.*

GEORGE (*shouting*): What bloody mouse? (*Pause.*) I'll kill him. I'll ram his policies and his third party fire and thefts down his throat. I'll fully comprehensively break his neck! She's married to me! I've got a paper to prove it! (*Sadly:*) But there's nothing in the small print to say she can't go off with anybody else.

Your Hair of Gold

GEORGE (*sings in the style of Jim Reeves*):
Your hair of gold, your eyes of baby blue —

How could I ever face a life without you?
Your lips so sweet, your touch so tender –
You know I surrender to everything that you do.

Your glance, your smile – they haunt me all the while:
Sleeping or waking you're always there beside me:
Your laugh, your kiss – my riches forever:
You know that I'll never let you go from my heart.

GEORGE *goes off as the lights go up to show* ADRIAN *standing in the hall.*

ADRIAN: My mother has arranged what she called a civilised meeting. Mr Lucas is going to be there. Naturally I am not invited. I'm going to listen at the door.

ADRIAN *listens at the living-room door. The lights go up in the living room to show* PAULINE, MR LUCAS *and* GEORGE *arguing.*

GEORGE *paces about, he looks haggard.* PAULINE *watches him anxiously.* MR LUCAS *starts talking.* GEORGE *hangs his head.* PAULINE *gets up to comfort him.* GEORGE *pushes her away. He takes a handkerchief out of his pocket and wipes his eyes.* PAULINE *talks, her eyes down.*

The civilised meeting broke up when my father found out how long my mother and Mr Lucas had been in love. And when my mother disclosed that she was leaving for Sheffield with Mr Lucas, my father became uncivilised and started fighting! In the *front* garden. All the neighbours came out to watch.

ADRIAN *runs up to the first floor.*

GEORGE *and* MR LUCAS *mime fighting.* PAULINE *mimes trying to break it up.* MR LUCAS *escapes into the front garden.* GEORGE *and* PAULINE *run after him.* ADRIAN *hangs out of the window, watching.*

GEORGE (*shouting*): You're not having her! She's my wife!
He rugby tackles MR LUCAS *and brings him down.*

PAULINE: Don't hurt him, George!

GEORGE: Hurt him – I'll kill him!
MR LUCAS *gets up and hits* GEORGE *on the jaw.*

PAULINE: Don't hurt him, Bimbo!

MR LUCAS: She belongs to me now!
PAULINE *gets between the two but is unable to stop* GEORGE *head butting* MR LUCAS.

PAULINE: It was supposed to be a civilised meeting.
GEORGE *and* MR LUCAS *stagger in opposite directions.*

MR LUCAS: Ah! He's hurt me, Pauline! He's broken my nose. I shall look like Henry Cooper.

PAULINE: Go on! Finish each other off! Kill him, George! Get stuck in! You're uncivilised, the pair of you!

MR LUCAS: Steady on Pauline.

GEORGE *chases* MR LUCAS *off.*

PAULINE (*distraught*): I don't care any more. I'm going to Sheffield, with him or without him. (*Screaming*:) I can see you looking through your net curtains, Mrs O'Leary!

PAULINE *runs off.*

ADRIAN (*from the front bedroom window*): All the people looked up and saw me so I looked especially sad. I expect the experience will give me a trauma at some stage in the future. I'm all right at the moment, but you never know.

The lights go up to show GEORGE *in the bathroom bathing his face, and* PAULINE *in the bedroom packing a suitcase.* ADRIAN *is in his bedroom with the dog.*

Family Trio

ADRIAN (*sings*): Two o'clock in the morning:
Leicester's asleep as sound as a log:
I count sheep in the stillness,
As we lie awake — just me and the dog.

PAULINE (*sings*): Maybe this is the right time to
Find out what I am good for,
And what would be really good for me —
Maybe . . . maybe
I'm more, more than I bargained for,
Braver than I believed I could
Be — I'm free to become . . . who knows?
We'll see, maybe . . .

GEORGE (*sings*): Your hair of gold, your eyes of baby blue —
How could I ever face a life without you?

ADRIAN (*sings*): Five o'clock in the morning:
No one's about, not even a mouse:
All peace and quiet on the outside —
Who would believe there's a war in our house?

PAULINE (*sings*): GEORGE (*sings simultaneously with* PAULINE):

Maybe this is the right time to Your hair of gold, your eyes of
Find out what I am good for, baby blue—
And what would be really How could I ever face a life
good for me without you?
Maybe . . . maybe Your lips so sweet, your touch
I'm more, more than I so tender —

  bargained for,   You know I surrender to
Braver than I believed I could   everything that you do.
Be — I'm free to become . . .
  who cares?
We'll see, maybe . . .

ADRIAN (*sings, as* GEORGE *and* PAULINE *repeat their verses*):
  Five o'clock in the morning:
  No one's about, not even a mouse:
  Nothing moves in the silence —
  Who would believe there's a war in our house?

ADRIAN/PAULINE/GEORGE (*sing*):
  Maybe . . . maybe . . . maybe . . . maybe . . . we'll see.
  Blackout.

ACT TWO

ADRIAN *is in his bedroom writing in his diary.* GEORGE *is downstairs in the living-room slumped on the sofa. He is unshaven.*

ADRIAN (*voice over*): Tuesday March 31st. My mother has gone to Sheffield with Mr Lucas. She had to drive because Mr. Lucas couldn't see out of his black eyes. I have informed the school secretary of my mother's desertion, she was very kind and gave me a form to give to my father; it is for free school dinners. We are now a single parent family. Nigel has asked Barry Kent to stop menacing me for a few weeks. Barry Kent said he would think about it.

ADRIAN *comes downstairs and sits down opposite* GEORGE.

GEORGE: I don't know what I did wrong. I never hit her. I was tempted, but I never actually got round to (GEORGE *punches the air viciously, landing a blow.*) I put my money on the table every Friday night without fail; not all, but most. I've got a temper (*Losing his temper.*) all right, I admit it! It's a fault I've got *and* I shout a bit, but I mean nothing by it. (*Calmer.*) I thought she'd got used to it. Has she gone because I'm losing my hair? (*Pause.*) I know I've let myself go downhill. — No I've not, she has. She stopped sewing my buttons on and stitching my turnups. And I can't remember the last time she bought me any Cherry Blossom. They've noticed at work; a memo was passed about my shoes. When you tell the punters how much the storage heater'll cost, they look on the floor. You can lose a sale because of the lack of a good shine. (*Pause.*) I know things weren't too hot physically, but it was her fault! She put a barrier between us. She read the *Guardian* in bed at night. Even worse, she even sometimes read bits out! 'Listen to what Jill Tweedie says about men' — she'd say. It was never complimentary. It's Jill Tweedie's fault that Pauline's gone. Her and that Greasy Greer! (*Pause.*) So why's she gone off with *another man*?

GRANDMA *enters, taking her hat and coat off.*

GRANDMA: Hello, Adrian, you look pale. You're not constipated are you? I've got a bottle of syrup of figs in my bag if you are.

ADRIAN: No, it's all right. I went this morning.

GRANDMA: Good boy. Where's Pauline, George?

GEORGE *and* ADRIAN *exchange a glance.*

GEORGE: She's in Sheffield.

GRANDMA: Who does she know in Sheffield?

GEORGE: Mr Lucas from next door.

GRANDMA: But Mr Lucas from next door lives next door, doesn't he?

GEORGE: No, not any more he doesn't. He lives in Sheffield — with Pauline.

GRANDMA: Do you mean that they're living . . . together?

GEORGE: Yes.

GRANDMA: In sin?

GEORGE: Yes.

GRANDMA: I knew it! I always said she was wanton. Thank the good Lord your father never lived to see this day. It would have killed him.
She sits. ADRIAN *goes off to fetch the tea things.*

GEORGE: It's hit me hard, Mum.

GRANDMA: How she could bear to tear herself away from that wonderful boy? It just proves how inhuman she is.

GEORGE: I keep seeing them together, in Sheffield . . . making love in front of a knife and fork factory.

GRANDMA: You're well rid of her, George. She never cleaned behind the cooker.

GEORGE: I should have taken her out more. She loved Chinese food. The odd prawn ball wouldn't have hurt me.
ADRIAN *enters carrying a tea tray with milk carton, sugar bag, mugs and a packet of biscuits.*

GRANDMA (*to* ADRIAN): What's that supposed to be?

ADRIAN: It's the tea tray, Grandma.

GRANDMA: I'll excuse you this once, Adrian, it must have been unsettling when your mother left home. But it's no good descending to the level of animals. Now, go back into the kitchen and do it properly; milk jug, sugar bowl, doily for the biscuits, cups and saucers and apostle spoons.
ADRIAN *goes out to the kitchen with the tray.*
How's *he* taken it?

GEORGE: I don't know he's not said. I can still smell her perfume on the sheets!
GEORGE *starts to sniffle.*

GRANDMA: Right. I'll have *them* in the wash tomorrow. Now, go upstairs and have a shave. You may think it's amusing to look like a Communist but I don't. I know you've had a bit of a shock . . .

GEORGE: A bit of a shock! My world has fallen apart! I'm a broken man!
GEORGE *cries.*

GRANDMA: You've no gumption, George. Your father shaved every day of his life. Even when he was in the trenches at Ypres. Sometimes he had to stop the rats from eating his shaving soap. He was even shaved in his coffin by the undertaker, so if the dead can shave, then there's no excuse for the living.

GEORGE: I don't want to go on living, not without Pauline. I love her, Mum.

GRANDMA: Do you want me to smack your bum? You might be forty-one but you're not too old. I won't have you giving way to your emotions like this — it's not healthy. All this silly slobber about *love*. It's decency that counts. Keeping a clean front and paying your bills on time. Where's love got you, eh? I shall leave the room until you've pulled yourself together. (*Pause.*)
GRANDMA *goes off to the kitchen. Lights on kitchen.*
ADRIAN *is pouring sugar into a bowl.*

GRANDMA: I'm sorry to see your father in such a state.

ADRIAN: He found one of my mother's earrings down the back seat of the car this morning. He kept staring at it with a funny look in his eyes . . . Then he asked me if I missed my mother. I said 'Of course I do, but life must go on!'

GRANDMA: Quite right.

ADRIAN: But *he* said: 'I don't see why.' I took this to mean that he was suicidal. So I took his razor and all the sleeping pills from out of the bathroom. Just to be on the safe side.

GRANDMA: Good boy.
They enter the living-room.
It's times like this I realise what a privilege it was to be married to your grandad. There was no suicide threats or adultery in *our* marriage. We just plodded on day after day for forty years. I wouldn't say we were especially happy, but then again we weren't unhappy either. Your grandad was a quiet man; he hated noise and disagreements, so there were no rows. But I knew when he was upset; he used to rap his fingers on the mangle outside the back door. (*She demonstrates on the coffee table.*)

ADRIAN: Yes, he used to do that a lot when I came round.

GRANDMA: Yes, well you used to get on his nerves a bit — always asking questions.

ADRIAN: He never answered any.

GRANDMA: How could he? He didn't know anything. I used to read bits out of the newspaper to him sometimes, but he'd say: 'Don't bother me with the outside world, May.' It upset him, you see. I suppose you could say he was a timid man.

Your Dead Grandad

GRANDMA (*sings*): I don't recall
Just when he popped the question:
I'm not exactly sure he ever did!
He bought a ring – I've still got that:
We hired a hall, he hired a top hat –
He looked a toff, your dead Grandad.

ADRIAN: Can I have a biscuit please Grandma?

GRANDMA (*sings*): He never had to tell me that he loved me –
We had no use for sentimental chat:
I'd wash the dishes – he would dry,
We dug the garden – time passed by:
I miss him still, your dead Grandad.

ADRIAN: Grandma, can I . . .?
ADRIAN *reaches for a biscuit.* GRANDMA *slaps his hand.*

GRANDMA (*sings*): We never made excuses for bad manners,
No psycho-this or socio-that at all:
Folks were either sane or mad,
We'd no posh words for being bad –
But he was good, your dead Grandad.

George!

GEORGE: Yes, Mum.

GRANDMA: Would you mind driving me up to the Garden Centre in the car? Only I'm running low on poisons.

GEORGE (*getting the coats*): No – I don't mind.

GRANDMA: Good, and it'll take you out of yourself, won't it? Do you want to come, Adrian?

ADRIAN: I'd love to but Nigel's coming round to collect a book.

GRANDMA: (*kissing* ADRIAN): Well, bye bye love. And don't fret about your mother. You know what they say: 'The bad penny gathers no moss.'
NIGEL *enters as* GRANDMA *and* GEORGE *go off.*

GEORGE: Go through, he's in there.

ADRIAN: Oh you're here.

NIGEL: Yeah, you got it?

ADRIAN: Yes.

He takes a magazine called Big and Bouncy *from under a cushion and gives it to* NIGEL, *who flicks through it and puts it under his jumper.*

NIGEL: God, your furniture! It's like reject corner at MFI in here. I get a shock everytime I come in.

ADRIAN: I know. (*Apologetically.*) It was brilliant staying at your house last weekend, Nigel. It's really opened my eyes. Without knowing it I've been living in poverty for the last fourteen years. Perhaps if *my* father had built a formica cocktail cabinet in *our* lounge, my mother would still be here.

NIGEL: I doubt it. Your mum left because your dad went round looking like a scruffbag. You can't expect a woman to put up with it. In fact, Adrian, if you don't do something about your own personal image, you're going to end up sentenced to a life of chastity.

Get It Right!

NIGEL (*sings*): Adrian Mole, why d'you look such a right arsehole?
I've never seen anyone dress worse!
Your bottoms are flared and your boots curl up like
   they're scared
And your duffel coat positively festers!
Your jumper is straight off the tip —
Do you wear it in bed when you kip?
Oh Moley, you're wholly, completely — words defeat me!
Try Lacoste, Doc Martens, some Farahs you'd look smart in —
If you want to wear clothes — get them right!

Your bike's a disgrace — you need a BMX or a racer
With a speedo and ten gears like my one:
This Walkman will surprise you, got a built-in graphic equaliser
With these new lightweight 'phones — why not try one?
This digital Seiko's for you
If you want to play chess in the loo:
Oh, Mole-face, it's as simple as squeezing a pimple!
Ask for Raleigh, or Sony, Ticini, Cerutti —
Whatever you get — get it right!

Your taste, I must say, falls far short of a true gourmet —
You live on baked beans and fish fingers:
In a hurry a curry from a tin saves a lot of worry,
But it does have a strong pong that lingers:

The best things are subtle, not loud,
And known to a few, not the crowd:
Not your Tizer from Tesco — Frascati, *al fresco*!
Say Martini, say Campari, say Adidas, say Atari,
Say Honda, Sekonda, aerobics, Jane Fonda —
If you want to get on — get it right!

Anyway, must rush, I'm seeing Pandora at 4 o'clock.
We're having wholemeal crumpets in front of the log fire.

ADRIAN: You're dead lucky Nigel. What's she like to go out with?

NIGEL: To tell you the truth she's not much cop. I'm used to birds that give it out, talking of which have you heard from your mum?

ADRIAN: I had a postcard telling me that she'd found a flat — she lives at 69a President Carter Walk, Sheffield. Why can't she write a letter like any normal person? Why should the postman be able to read my confidential business? I've asked my father if I can go.

NIGEL: What's he say?

ADRIAN (*imitating* GEORGE): Yeah, providing she sends the train fare.
ADRIAN *moves off stage.*

ADRIAN (*voice over*): It was the first time I'd been on a train on my own. I'm certainly spreading my wings lately. (*Pause.*) Sheffield looks just like Leicester really. I didn't see any knife and fork factories. So I suppose Margaret Thatcher has closed them all down.
PAULINE *and* MR LUCAS's *Sheffield flat.*
ADRIAN *and* PAULINE *come in with shopping. They are met by* MR LUCAS.

MR LUCAS: Had a good day?
He goes to PAULINE *and kisses her then puts his arms around her from the back. He almost touches her breasts but* PAULINE *holds his hands firmly.*

PAULINE: *I* did. (*To* ADRIAN:) Did you, love?

ADRIAN: Yes, thank you.

PAULINE: There's no need to be so polite! I'm your mother — remember?

MR LUCAS: What did you get up to then, young Adrian?
ADRIAN *turns away from* MR LUCAS.

ADRIAN: We had a Chinese Businessman's lunch, then we went to Habitat to buy a lampshade for . . . (*He looks at* PAULINE.)

PAULINE: Our bedroom. Then we saw a Monty Python film — it was all about the life of Jesus.

ADRIAN (*to* PAULINE): I felt guilty laughing!

PAULINE: And I got him some nice new trousers — tight ones!
MR LUCAS *kisses* PAULINE's *hair, neck and lips.*

PAULINE: Don't! (*She pushes* MR LUCAS *away.*)

ADRIAN: I'm going to try my new trousers on.

PAULINE: All right, love.
ADRIAN *goes off.*

MR LUCAS: Did you notice? He didn't look me in the eye once.

PAULINE: He's bound to feel a bit strange. I do myself.
MR LUCAS *grabs* PAULINE.

Oh let go of me! I'm fed up with you mauling me about.
I feel like the last chicken in Sainsbury's! How would you feel if a man was messing about with your mother?

MR LUCAS: I'd be very surprised. She's been dead for five years.

PAULINE: There's so much I don't know about you. The false teeth came as a surprise.

MR LUCAS: I've only got the four.

PAULINE: Yes, but at the front. Don't take them out again, will you? Not at bed time.

MR LUCAS: I'm glad you brought up the subject of bed time. When do you think we'll be able to — er — get together?

PAULINE (*pause*): I can't. I just can't. Not with that child here.

MR LUCAS: But it's our honeymoon, Paulie.

PAULINE: Would you mind not calling me 'Paulie'? It reminds me of childhood illnesses. My name's *Pauline*, Derek.

MR LUCAS: Oh, I see. So it's Derek now is it, Mrs Mole?

PAULINE: Yes and I don't think it will ever be Mrs Pauline Lucas either.

MR LUCAS: But you promised to marry me! You said you'd get a divorce. You've been using me. Oh God, I feel dirty!

PAULINE: Oh try and pull yourself together, Derek. You sound like something out of Barbara Cartland!
ADRIAN *enters. He is wearing tight black trousers. The labels are hanging off.*

MR LUCAS: Who's a super trendy, then?

PAULINE: Oh you do look nice, Adrian. They really suit you. Turn round. Doesn't he look grown up!
ADRIAN *turns.*

MR LUCAS: Oh yes, the birds will be after you now, eh Adrian?
ADRIAN *blushes, looks uncomfortable.*

ADRIAN: Can you take the labels off please, Mum?

MR LUCAS (*taking a Swiss army knife out of his apron pocket*): Allow me. Don't know how I survived without my Swiss army knife. Now, where's the scissors? (*He fumbles with the blades.*) 'Course they're wasted on the Swiss − never fought a decent war. (*Still fumbling.*) Very good for emergencies.
ADRIAN *and* PAULINE *watch as he fumbles.*

PAULINE: Slow emergencies.

MR LUCAS: Give me a chance, Pauline! (*Still fumbling.*) You can saw through a tree with a Swiss army knife, Adrian. In fact, we'll have a drive out to the countryside tomorrow and I'll prove it to you.

ADRIAN (*coldly*): It's against the law to saw trees down.

MR LUCAS: Bloody bureaucrats!

PAULINE: Yes, it'll do us all good to get out of here and get some fresh air in our lungs. (*She rips the labels from* ADRIAN's *trousers with her bare hands.*)

MR LUCAS (*handing the Swiss army knife to* ADRIAN): I want you to have this, Adrian. As a sort of memento of your visit which sincerely I hope will be the first of many. We both want you to regard this as your second home.

PAULINE: Oh Bimbo, what a lovely thing to do.

ADRIAN: Sorry, but I can't accept it. I've turned pacifist.

MR LUCAS (*martyred*): I don't mind admitting I'm very, very hurt. I would have given an arm and a leg for one of these when I was a lad.
He goes off.

PAULINE: Adrian − why didn't you accept it graciously? He's trying ever so hard to be nice to you.

ADRIAN: Mum, there's things you ought to know about Creep Lucas.

PAULINE: What?

ADRIAN: There's a new family moved into his house and the bloke, Mr Singh, he found this stack of horrible magazines under the lino in the bathroom.

PAULINE: So?

ADRIAN: Well, they belonged to Mr Lucas. He's a pervert! You'll have to come home.

PAULINE: What were these magazines called?

ADRIAN: *Amateur Photographer*.

PAULINE: So, Bimbo's interested in photography — it doesn't mean he's Jack the Ripper!

ADRIAN: Mum you'll have to come home soon. Dad's falling in love with another woman.

PAULINE: What's her name?

ADRIAN: Doreen Slater.

PAULINE (*laughs*): Oh — Dopey Doreen! Is she still making the rounds? My god, she's got some staying power!
PAULINE *goes off.* ADRIAN *goes to his house. He goes upstairs and looks at* GEORGE's *bed.*

ADRIAN (*voice over*): My father said he had had Doreen Slater to tea. By the state of the house I should think he'd had her for breakfast, dinner and tea! I have never seen the woman, but from the evidence she left behind, I know she has got bright red hair, wears orange lipstick and sleeps on the left side of the bed. What a homecoming!

BERT BAXTER's *house.* BERT *is in his chair. Toothless.*

BERT (*looking for his teeth*): Where are yer? Where are yer? (*Shouting to* ADRIAN *off:*) I know I 'ad 'em this mornin' but then I took 'em out to give me gums a rest. I've looked in the lavvy but they're not on the window sill where I usually leaves 'em.
ADRIAN *enters.*

ADRIAN: I wish you hadn't rung me at school, Bert. I got into trouble. Scruton went mad.

BERT: Scruton? That the headmaster? Stuck-up git! I told *him* a few things. You haven't found 'em, then?

ADRIAN: No, I've looked everywhere.

BERT: I shall have to find 'em. They've got sentimental value: belonged to me father. I've had them teeth since 1946 and besides I shall starve. I can't chew me beetroot. 'Ave another look, there's a good lad. And see how Sabre is will you? He's been quiet all morning. It ain't like 'im.

ADRIAN: He's chewing something in his kennel. He's all right.
ADRIAN *goes off.*
BERT *is struggling to get out of his chair but can't do it.*

BERT (*to his legs*): Come on me old beauties. Don't let me down! (*He sits back.*)

ADRIAN *enters with* BERT*'s teeth held between thumb and finger.*

BERT: You've found 'em! Good lad. Where was they?

ADRIAN: In Sabre's kennel.

BERT (*laughs*): He's a bugger! Give 'em a swill under the tap.

ADRIAN (*horrified*): Bert, no!

BERT: I can't put 'em straight back into me mouth after a dog's been chewing 'em all night, can I? What's up with you, ain't you heard of hygiene?
ADRIAN *goes out to* BERT's *kitchen.*
Talking of which, ain't it time you came round and did a bit o' cleaning'? Tomorrow will be all right.
ADRIAN *comes back, drying the teeth on a tea towel.*

ADRIAN: I can't come tomorrow, my mother's coming home to talk about who gets custody.

BERT: Who gets the custard?

ADRIAN: *Custody*, Bert.
He gives BERT *the teeth.* BERT *puts them into his mouth.*
(*To the audience:*) This is the most revolting thing I have ever seen, and I'm no stranger to squalor.

BERT: Be a good lad an' make me a beetroot sandwich up will you?

ADRIAN: OK.
ADRIAN *makes a sandwich.*

BERT: So, your mum and dad are gettin' a divorce are they?

ADRIAN (*sadly*): Yes.

BERT: I don't hold with divorce. I was married for thirty-five miserable years, so why should anybody else get away with it? (*Pause.*) Did I ever show you a photo of my wife?

ADRIAN: No, Bert.

BERT: Pass us the photo album then. It's in the pouffee.
ADRIAN *passes the album.*
(*Opening the album.*) That's her. (*Pause.*) 'Course it were in the days before they had plastic surgery. (*Pause.*)

ADRIAN: She looks a bit like . . .

BERT: An 'oss? Yes, I know, funny that. I never realised until I stopped working with 'osses and went to work on the railways.

ADRIAN: I'd better go now, Bert.

BERT: No, stay a bit longer, lad. Here — you seen this Bible? Save my life this did. I had it in me breast pocket when a Jerry sniper shot at me. See that? It's a bullet hole. Saved my life. It was a miracle!

ADRIAN: But this Bible was printed in 1958, Bert.

BERT: Well, I said it was a miracle!

   BERT *goes out.* ADRIAN *crosses to the Mole living-room.*

GEORGE MOLE *is hoovering the living-room. He is singing 'Your Hair of Gold'. He is looking cheerful. He's tidied himself up.*

GEORGE: Adrian, I'm just off to fetch your mother's flowers. Won't be long. Carry on cleaning up.

   ADRIAN *makes sure that his father has gone then he takes a tape measure and looks round furtively. He takes a tiny notebook out and measures his thing and records the measurement. An Electricity Board* OFFICIAL *starts banging on the front door.* ADRIAN *drops the tape measure. He quickly adjusts his dress. He lets the* OFFICIAL *in.*

OFFICIAL: Electricity Board. You owe us £97.79.

ADRIAN: That's a lot.

OFFICIAL: Yes, it is isn't it? And it's obviously more than you can pay. So, I've come to cut you off. (*He enters the hall.*)

ADRIAN: But you can't do that! We need electricity for life's essentials, like the television and stereo!

OFFICIAL (*opening his tool box*): It's people like you what are sapping the country's strength. Where's the meter cupboard?

ADRIAN: There.

   The OFFICIAL *goes to the cupboard and fiddles around. The Mole lights go down.*

OFFICIAL (*mournfully*): Do you think I enjoy doing this son?

   The OFFICIAL *puts his hand on* ADRIAN*'s shoulder.*

ADRIAN: No, I'm sure you don't.

OFFICIAL: Well you'd be wrong because I do! Good morning.

   GEORGE *enters. His arms full of flowers. He passes the* OFFICIAL.

GEORGE: Morning. Would you like a cup of tea?

OFFICIAL: No thank you, sir. I never fraternise with the enemy.

   He leaves.

GEORGE (*laughs*): It's nice to know that officials have got a sense of humour (*To* ADRIAN.) Stick these in a milk bottle, I'll finish the hoovering — she'll be here soon. (*He switches the Hoover on. No power.*) What the bloody hell's up with this? (*He kicks the Hoover.*) Have you been playing at Daleks again?

ADRIAN: No. Dad . . . we've been cut off. You haven't paid the bill. You should have put it away every week, in a jug, like Grandma does.

GEORGE: She'll be here soon and I've still got bits on my shag pile! You should have refused entry, you stupid . . . (*He swears under his breath.*)
MR LUCAS *enters.*

PAULINE (*shouting*): George! Adrian!

GEORGE: Pauline! Love, you look wonderful!
MR LUCAS *enters.*
What's he doing here? I thought Adrian's custody was being decided between the two of us?

MR LUCAS: Where Pauline goes, I go.

PAULINE: It's gloomy in here, George. Can't we have a light on?

ADRIAN: No. We've had our electricity cut off.

GEORGE: Temporarily.

PAULINE (*kindly*): Well, I'm not surprised you can't pay the bills, George — these flowers must have cost a fortune.

MR LUCAS: If you want to borrow a ton, George . . .

GEORGE: All I want from you, Lucas, is my wife.

PAULINE: But apart from having no electricity, you're keeping the house beautifully, George.
MR LUCAS *offers* ADRIAN *a fiver.*

MR LUCAS: Here, Adrian, go and buy some candles. This meeting might go on all night. We can't negotiate in the dark.

ADRIAN: Shall I, Dad?

GEORGE: We've got no choice, son. I'm skint.
ADRIAN *goes to his room. The lights go down on the living-room and up on* ADRIAN's *bedroom.*

ADRIAN (*voice over*): The arguing went on for ages. In fact until it was time to light the candles. Mr Lucas spilt candle wax on his new shoes. It was the only cheerful incident in a tragic day.
PAULINE *walks off followed by* MR LUCAS.
GEORGE MOLE *is talking on the phone to* DOREEN SLATER.

GEORGE: Doreen, I know I said it was all over. But I can't stop thinking about you . . . Baby. Thanks, warm the bed up.
GEORGE *puts the phone down, grabs the flowers and goes out quickly.*

Dog
(*'The House Where I Live' reprise*)

ADRIAN (*sits on the bed and sings to the dog*):
> You are my only true friend,
> Always here at the end
> Of a traumatic day:
> I'm used to your slobb'ring embrace
> And your lop-sided face . . . is okay.
>
> Oh Dog, never gave you a name,
> Still I'm glad that you came
> To the house where I live.
>
> You are so easy to please
> And occasional fleas
> Don't detract from your charms:
> I s'pose you're a bit of a mess,
> But I couldn't care less − in my arms,
>
> Oh Dog, you're so floppy and warm!
> We'll both weather the storm
> In the house where we live.

The candlelit living-room. GEORGE *and* ADRIAN *are sitting around a small primus stove. They are wearing scarves and gloves.* GEORGE *is reading* Playboy. ADRIAN *is reading a hardback book, using a torch.*

GEORGE: What's that you're reading?

ADRIAN: *Hard Times* by Charles Dickens.

GEORGE: D'you want some more beans, son? (*He hands him a Heinz tin and spoon.*)

ADRIAN: No thanks, I don't like them cold.

GEORGE: Y'know this is good training for when civilisation collapses. You'll thank me one day.

ADRIAN: Oh, I don't mind. In fact, it's quite nice. (*Pause.*) Dad, what do you think my chances are of becoming a vet?

GEORGE: Nil. (*a*) You're no good at Science.
(*b*) You don't want to be a vet, son, they spend half their live with their hands stuck up cows' bums.
A noise off.
GRANDMA *enters the house, she gropes about in the dark.*

GRANDMA: George, are you there?

GEORGE: Blow the candles out! It's your Grandma!

ADRIAN: She's bound to find us, Dad. We may as well surrender.
ADRIAN *goes to* GRANDMA*'s aid.*

GRANDMA (*trying to switch the lights on*): George! I know
you're there, I can hear voices.

ADRIAN: In here, Grandma!
GRANDMA *gropes into the room.*

GRANDMA: Whose idea was it to sit in the dark?

ADRIAN: The Electrity Board's.

GRANDMA: So, you've stopped paying your bills now, have you?

GEORGE: Pauline managed the money. I don't know how to do
it, Mum.

GRANDMA: It's quite simple. All you do is put it away in jugs.
Gas in a pink jug. Electricity in a blue and so on. How much
do you owe?

ADRIAN: Ninety-seven pounds seventy-nine pence.

GRANDMA: My god! Ninety-seven pounds. You must have a
leak somewhere! I'll call the Board out first thing tomorrow.
GRANDMA *takes a cheque book out of her bag and writes a
cheque by candlelight.*

ADRIAN (*in a loud whisper*): You shouldn't be taking money
from a pensioner.
GEORGE *hits* ADRIAN *round the head.*

GRANDMA: Now I shan't be able to re-stock my freezer. You
know I like to buy half a cow a year.
GRANDMA *gives* GEORGE *a cheque.*

GEORGE: I'm sorry, Mum. Thank you. I'll pay you back.

GRANDMA (*to* ADRIAN): Now what's this I hear about Barry
Kent beating you up for money?

ADRIAN: Who told you?

GRANDMA: It's all round the Evergreen Club.

GEORGE: I've been to see his father. But he wouldn't listen.
I daren't push it any further, he's like an ape, Mum. He's got
more hair on his knuckles than I've got on my head.

GRANDMA: Where does this Barry Kent boy live?

ADRIAN: Number Thirteen Corporation Row. You're not
thinking of going are you?
ADRIAN *stands.*

GEORGE: Leave it to the police, Mum.
GEORGE *stands.*

GRANDMA (*with contempt*): The police! We Moles fight our
own battles! (*She straightens her back and leaves.*)
GEORGE *goes off.*

ADRIAN (*to the audience*): She was gone one hour and seven
minutes. She came in, took her coat off. Fluffed her hair
out. Took £27.18 from the anti-mugger belt around her
waist. She said 'He won't bother you again, Adrian, but if he
does, let me know'. Then she got the tea ready, pilchards,
tomatoes and ginger cake. I bought her a box of diabetic
chocolates from the chemists as a token of my esteem.

Lights go up in the kitchen where DOREEN SLATER *is making
tea.*

ADRIAN (*voice over*): My father rang Doreen Slater up and
asked her to come round. It was quite a shock to see her for
the first time. Why my father wants to have carnal knowledge
of her I can't imagine. She is as thin as a stick insect. She has
got no bust and no bum. She is just straight all the way up and
all the way down.
The phone rings. DOREEN, *picks up the phone in the hall.*
PAULINE *in a housecoat on the other side of the stage is
holding a phone.*

DOREEN: Hello, George Mole's residence.

PAULINE: To whom am I speaking at 7.30 in the morning?

DOREEN: I'm Miss Doreen Slater. To whom am *I* speaking?

PAULINE: Mrs Pauline Mole. Could I speak to my son please?

DOREEN: I don't know if he's up. I've only just got out of
bed myself.

PAULINE: Out of my husband's bed, I presume?
ADRIAN *comes downstairs.*

DOREEN: I don't see what it's got to do with you. You're the
one that left. You've upset me now. (*To* ADRIAN:) Your
mother's on the phone.
ADRIAN *grabs the phone.*

ADRIAN: Mum?

PAULINE: What's Doreen Slater doing in *my* house?

ADRIAN: Dad sent for her. Something terrible's happened.

PAULINE: It's not the dog?

ADRIAN: No, it's Dad. He's been made redundant from his
job. He'll be on the dole! Mum — how will we manage on the
pittance the Government gives us? The dog will have to go.
It costs thirty-five pence a day, not counting Winalot! Mum —
I'm now a single parent child with a father on the dole. Social
Security will be buying my shoes!

PAULINE: Calm down, Adrian. I'll buy your shoes. Oh my god, what next? How's he taken it?

ADRIAN: He's having a nervous breakdown I think. He watches *Playschool*!

PAULINE: That's nothing to worry about. He's always watched *Playschool* when he got the chance. (*Fondly:*) He used to love guessing the shape of the windows. Oh, I wish I were there right now.

ADRIAN: So do I, Mum. Come home.

PAULINE: I can't Adrian. I haven't found what I'm looking for yet. 'Bye pet.
The lights go down on PAULINE. *She goes off.*

DOREEN: Well, what's happening? Is she coming home or what? Only I need to know. I'm having a new fireplace put in at my home.

ADRIAN: She's not coming back. (*He puts the phone down.*)

DOREEN: So does that mean I'm staying, then?

ADRIAN: I don't know. You'd better ask my dad.

DOREEN: Only if I knew, I could cancel the fireplace.

ADRIAN: Hasn't *he* said anything?

DOREEN: No, he doesn't talk. He doesn't do anything and I mean anything. He's been rendered impotent.
ADRIAN *blanches.*
He was all right before he was made redundant. He was ever so good at it — you don't mind me talking like this, do you? No, of course you don't. In my day, adults didn't talk about . . . you know . . . (*She mouths 'sex'.*) But now, it's all open and above board, isn't it? You and your mates talk about it all the time, don't you?
ADRIAN *shakes his head.*
Have you noticed how much he's drinking and smoking?
ADRIAN *nods.*

ADRIAN: Yes, I think he's going mental.

DOREEN: I'm ever so worried about him, he's not sleeping either, he just lies in bed with his arms folded behind his head, staring at the ceiling. People are talking about me you know. Saying I've got no morals. It's because my Maxwell was born out of wedlock. But it's not my fault, is it? I'd give anything to be *in* wedlock. It's just my bad luck that I fall in love with married men. (*Pause.*) Over and over again.
ADRIAN *looks on with growing distaste.*

The Other Woman

DOREEN (*sings*): The other woman — *his* other woman:
I'm another woman in the hours he spends with me:
'The other woman' — why does it bother me?
You'd think by now I'd play my old familiar role with some
  good grace.

Now, for a week or two,
I'll pretend he'll stay with me —
Such hurried ecstacy!
Then she'll reappear, he'll say 'Sorry, my dear, it was fun' —
And out will go the sun.

The other woman: who *is* 'the other woman'?
Who has shown concern for him? Deserves his trust and love?
The other woman, *this* other woman,
While she ran out on him, without a thought, without a
  backward glance:

Who came to rescue him,
Soothed away all his pain,
Made him feel brave again?
This other woman, who secretly knew from the start
That he would break my heart.

DOREEN *goes upstairs.*

ADRIAN (*to the audience*): Doreen talks to me as if I was
another adult instead of her lover's son, aged fourteen, two
months and one day. I'm just about sick of so-called adults.
You would think that they would be old enough to manage
their lives a bit better, but oh, no! They go about baring
their sickly emotions to anybody who will listen. All this
family trouble is sending me rebellious. In fact, I wore red
socks to school. It's strictly forbidden but I don't care any
more.
ADRIAN *shows his red socks to the audience then walks to
the school wall.* ADRIAN *stands between* PANDORA,
NIGEL *and another schoolgirl showing his red socks.*
NIGEL's *trousers are tucked into his socks.* PANDORA's
socks are lurex.

PANDORA: You're a true revolutionary, Adrian. When they
come to write the history of school politics — your name will
be in the index under 'M'.

NIGEL: I was gob-smacked when I heard it was you who lead the
revolt — I didn't think you were the revolting type!

ADRIAN: Well, I'm not really — in fact I can't help wishing that
I'd worn my black socks the other day.

PANDORA: Come on now, Adrian — no revisionism. Stand by
your principles! Why should we be forced to wear the black
socks of oppression?

NIGEL: Come on then! Let's march on Scruton's office!

ADRIAN: But what if the GCE examiners find out about it next
year? It could jeopardise our 'O' levels!

NIGEL: He's got a point — a valid one.

PANDORA: So am I going to face that fascist pig Scruton on my
own?

ADRIAN: No, I'll come with you. I've started — so I'll finish. Are
you coming, Nigel?

NIGEL: It's a moral decision, isn't it?

SCHOOLGIRL: Yes it is, darling.

NIGEL: It's a bit hard to know what to do.

PANDORA: If one's immoral — it's hard. But, if one has
principles — then one has no choice. *She starts to sing 'We
Shall Not Be Moved'. The* SCHOOLGIRL *and the* BOYS *join
in weakly but then with gathering strength. They march
towards* SCRUTON's *office. Enter* SCRUTON.

SCRUTON: Good morning.

KIDS (*together*): Good morning, sir!

SCRUTON: Yes. I saw you making your way down the school
drive. Very colourful, very foolhardy. What a brave little band
you are! Now I should like you to hear the letter which I shall
be sending to your parents.
'Dear Mr and Mrs . . .,
'It is my sad duty to inform you that your son — stroke —
daughter has deliberately flaunted one of the rules of this
school. I take an extremely serious view of this contravention.
I am, therefore, suspending your son — stroke — daughter for
a period of one week.

PANDORA: But, sir! What about our 'O' Levels . . .?

SCRUTON (*roaring*): QUIET!
Everyone jumps.

NIGEL: Can we wear our black socks with a red stripe, Sir?

SCRUTON (*roaring*): *No!* Your socks must be entirely,
absolutely, incontravertably dense, midnight, black!
SCRUTON *exits.*
PANDORA *starts to cry.*

ADRIAN: Now look what he's done. Don't cry, Pandora. Aren't
you going to try to stop her, Nigel?

NIGEL: No. She broke it off. She says I'm a philistine.
NIGEL *and the* SCHOOLGIRL *go off hand in hand.*
ADRIAN *pats* PANDORA's *shoulder.*

ADRIAN: Don't cry. I've had a rejection letter from the BBC.
Do you want to see it?
PANDORA *nods, she puts her head on* ADRIAN's *shoulder.*
He shows her the letter.
Music: 'Oh Pandora'.
PANDORA *and* ADRIAN *walk together.*

ADRIAN (*voice over*): Pandora and I are in love! It is official!
She told Claire Neilson who told Nigel who told me. I told
Claire to tell Pandora that I return her love. I can overlook
the fact that Pandora smokes five Benson and Hedges a day
and has her own lighter. When you are in love, such things
cease to matter!
ADRIAN *and* PANDORA *are sitting on a school bench in the
playground. They are not touching, but gazing into each
other's eyes. They hold hands.*

PANDORA: So, you didn't fall in love with me because of how I
look — like everybody else?

ADRIAN: Good god, no! That's dead sexist. No, it was because
of your personal integrity . . . and your brain.

PANDORA: But, you don't think I'm ugly do you?

ADRIAN: Ugly? You? You're Brillo Pad! You're the most
desirable, erotic girl I've ever clapped eyes on!

PANDORA: Do you want to kiss me?

ADRIAN: Well, of course I'd like to . . . I'm a bit out of
practice though . . .

PANDORA: Do you do French?

ADRIAN: Yes, I'm doing it for CSE.

PANDORA: French kissing!

ADRIAN: Oh no. I usually just stick to the English!
PANDORA *and* ADRIAN *fumble a kiss.* PANDORA *breaks
away.*

PANDORA: I don't think we're doing it properly. You need to
open your lips just a little wider, Adrian.

ADRIAN: Sorry.

PANDORA: Let's try again. (*They kiss.* PANDORA *breaks away.*)
Well, we've got plenty of time to practice. (*Pause.*) So *when*
did you fall in love with me?

ADRIAN: When I saw you playing netball.

PANDORA: I fell in love with your red socks first!

ADRIAN (*disappointed*): Oh . . .

PANDORA: Your socks were enormously significant. You see, I'm a radical and I'm going to devote my whole life to changing our spiritually bankrupt society.

ADRIAN: I'll help you if you like.

PANDORA: We can do it together!

ADRIAN: And when we're married . . .

PANDORA (*starting away*): Married! But we're only fourteen, darling.

ADRIAN (*laughing*): I know we can't get married now, thanks to the stupid adults that make the laws, but, in two years time . . .

PANDORA: We'll be sixteen.

ADRIAN: So we can get married. I know my Dad would give me permission — he can't wait for me to leave home and my mother's left home anyway, so she can't prevent us. Don't worry, I wouldn't stop you working . . . You could get a little job . . . something part-time . . . in a cake-shop, for instance. PANDORA *stands*.

PANDORA (*sternly*): *I* am going to Oxford University. While there, I may occasionally enter a cake shop, but I will be *buying* a granary loaf. I will certainly not be *selling* one!

ADRIAN: So you don't want to marry me and have twins?

PANDORA: I don't want to marry anybody!

ADRIAN: Not ever?

PANDORA: No! I shall live in sin.

ADRIAN: With me?

PANDORA: With several people I expect . . . in the course of a lifetime . . . *Music 'Oh Pandora'.*

During the song, ADRIAN *behaves like a Latin lover.*

Oh, Pandora

ADRIAN (*sings*): Oh, Pandora, I adore . . . ya:
From the first day that I saw ya
I felt destiny called,
I knew I was enthralled
By your aura of love — my Pandora!

Always wondered how it would be:
This is passion as it should be!
Your lips smoulder with fire,

> Your eyes melt with desire!
> Take me higher and higher, my Pandora!
>
> We'll get married straight away,
> Find a cottage by a stream
> With a private wishing-well
> Where I can dream
> Of my Pandora . . .

PANDORA (*sings*): Haven't done my physics homework:
> There's that film I want to see on El Salvador —
> It must be Channel Four:
> There's so much I have to do
> If I am to fulfil my potential —
> Musn't waste a second of my time!
>
> Get my 'O's and 'A's — then Oxford!
> Take a double first in Law and Economy —
> Dead right for an MP!
> Spare an afternoon a week
> For a lover or two, but no attachment,
> Nothing to deflect me from my course!

ADRIAN (*sings*):
> Two hearts beat in unison,
> Two souls joined in perfect
>   peace:

Our two bodies cry out loud	PANDORA (*sings simultaneously*
For release . . .	*with* ADRIAN):
Oh, please Pandora — I	Haven't done my physics
implore ya	homework:
From the first day that I	There's that film I want to see
saw ya	on El Salvador —
I felt destiny called,	It must be Channel Four.
I knew I was enthralled	There's so much I have to do
By your aura of love —	If I am to fulfil my potential –
my Pandora!	Mustn't waste a second of my
	time!
My Pandora,	Must go . . .
My Pandora,	Must go . . .
Oh, my Pandora!	Mustn't waste a second of my
	time!

PANDORA *leaves* ADRIAN *on his knees.*

ADRIAN (*voice over*): My precious love leaves these shores
    tomorrow. I am going to the airport to see her off. I hope her
    plane won't suffer from metal fatigue. I have just checked the
    world map to see where Tunisia is and I am most relieved to
    see that Pandora won't have to fly through the Bermuda Triangle.

ADRIAN *gets up and wanders about looking lost.*
(*To the audience*): Wednesday July 22nd! Why haven't I had a
postcard yet? What can have happened? Pandora! Pandora!
Pandora! (*He opens his notebook and clears his throat.*)
Oh! My love,
My heart is yearning
My mouth is dry,
My soul is burning.
You're in Tunisia
I am here.
Remember me and shed a tear.
Come back tanned and brown and healthy
You're lucky that your dad is wealthy.
She will be back in six days,
ADRIAN *writes in his diary.*
(*Voice over:*) Friday August 7th.
Moon's first quarter.
I rang Tunisia whilst my father was in the bath. He shouted
down to ask whom I was phoning. I told a lie. I said I was
phoning the speaking clock.
Pandora's flight left safely. She should be home around midnight.
'Oh Pandora' music triumphant. Enter PANDORA. *The lighting
becomes romantic. There is an emotional reunion with* ADRIAN.

PANDORA: Adrian!

ADRIAN: Pandora!
They embrace.
Did you have a good time?

PANDORA: No. It was dreadful. Mummy was bitten by a camel.
Then the Tunisian baggage handlers went on strike, but I told
you that on the phone. It *was* clever of you to ring me at
Tunis airport. Didn't your father mind?

ADRIAN: He doesn't know yet. I'm dreading the phone bill
coming.

PANDORA: We're together again — that's all that matters.
They start to leave.

ADRIAN (*to the audience*): Went to Pandora's house. Had an
emotional reunion behind her father's tool shed.
They go off.

ADRIAN (*voice over*): Monday October 5th.
Bert has been kidnapped by Social Services! They are keeping
him at the Alderman Cooper Sunshine Home. I have been to

see him. He shares a room with an old man called Thomas Bell. They have both got their names on their ashtrays. Sabre has got a place in the RSPCA hostel.

BERT *is sitting in a wheelchair looking miserable.*

MATRON *enters with* QUEENIE *in a wheelchair: An old lady with red hair and over-the-top make-up.*

MATRON: Mr Baxter, may I introduce a new guest to 'Smoker's Corner'?

BERT: Guest? It ain't an hotel you're runnin', Matron! It's an institution. What's run by the State. If I was a *guest* I could have my dog wi' me.

MATRON (*to* QUEENIE): Mr Baxter can be rather difficult, but we're hoping he will settle down. (*Pause.*) Most of our guests do. (*Pause.*) In time.

QUEENIE: Well, I think he's right. We're not guests, are we? None of us are here by choice. (*To* BERT): What's your name, love?

BERT: Bertram. What's yours?

QUEENIE: Queenie,

BERT *and* QUEENIE *look away from each other.*

MATRON: Well, you're getting on like a house on fire, aren't you? So, if you'll excuse me . . .

QUEENIE *and* BERT *stare hostilely at* MATRON *as she goes off.*

BERT: What you doin' in 'ere? You ain't incapable of lookin' after yourself, are you?

QUEENIE: Not in my opinion, I'm not. But I'm told that I'm going a bit doo-lally in the head.

BERT: Well, you seem all right to me.

QUEENIE: And to me. I think I've been put away because I like a drink now and again. You see, sometimes, after a drink, I forget where I am and I start singing.

BERT: What's wrong wi' that?

QUEENIE: I don't know. But others objected. Bus conductors and people in the library. D'you know what you've been put away for?

BERT: Yes. Me legs have gone.

QUEENIE: Shame, you're a fine figure of a man. (*Pause. She looks round.*) I don't like it in here, do you? It's full of old people!

BERT: I'm plannin' to escape.

QUEENIE: What, dig a tunnel?

BERT: No. I've got friends what are sortin' the paperwork out for me. It's only the paperwork what gets you out a' these places. Ay up there, Adrian! Ay up, Pandora!

ADRIAN: 'Lo Bert.

PANDORA *kisses* BERT.

PANDORA: How are you, darling?

BERT: I'm not happy and that's the truth.

ADRIAN: Cheer up, Bert. Russia's through to the European cup. BERT *cheers up.*

BERT: How's my Sabre?

ADRIAN: He's outside in the garden. Matron said he could cause heart failure amongst the guests.

BERT: I'm puttin' in an official complaint about *her*. Deprivin' a man of his liberty *and* his dog is unconstitutional.

PANDORA (*to* QUEENIE): Your hair is a lovely colour. What do you use?

QUEENIE: I do it once a week with six ounces of red henna. It's a big slice out me pension but I'd sooner go without food than have white hair. I haven't got the personality to be an old age pensioner. (*To* BERT:) Are you the only man in here?

BERT: Yes, I am.

PANDORA: Women live longer than men. It's a sort of bonus because we suffer more.

QUEENIE: I've hardly suffered at all. I've been happily married three times. All dead now, of course. But they died contented. ADRIAN *and* PANDORA *push* BERT *and* QUEENIE *in a wheelchair gavotte, during:*

The Young Girl Inside You

QUEENIE (*sings*): When you look in the mirror
The person reflected
Is a stranger you don't know
And don't care to meet:
But the young girl inside you
Is bright-eyed and flirty,
Not a day over thirty,
Who longs to be loved.

ADRIAN *and* PANDORA *dance the gavotte behind* BERT *and* QUEENIE.

Why does youth think it odd
That those older than God
Should know pangs of desire,

Feel the flame of love's fire?
It's not strange, it's not odd —
'Cause inside these old bodies
Our younger selves live
Just as lusty as you.

(*Wheelchair gavotte.*)

QUEENIE ⎰
BERT   ⎱ (*sing*): Why does youth think it odd
That those older than God
Should know pangs of desire,
Feel the flame of love's fire?
It's not strange, it's not odd —
'Cause inside these old bodies
Our younger selves live
Just as lusty as you.

QUEENIE: What am I doing in this thing? (*She gets out of her wheelchair.*)

PANDORA: You've got something for Bert, haven't you, Adrian?

BERT: Brought me some fags in, have you? Good lad. (*He holds his hand out expectantly.*)

ADRIAN: No, its a poem!

BERT (*disappointed*): Oh.

QUEENIE: How lovely! Read it out then.

ADRIAN: It's not very good.

BERT: Don't bother then.

PANDORA (*to* ADRIAN): Darling, you're too modest — go on.

ADRIAN: All right. (*He reads the poem.*)
Poem to Bert — by Adrian Mole.

Bert, you are dead old.
Fond of Sabre, beetroot and Woodbines
We have nothing in common,
I am fourteen and a half,
You are eighty-nine
You smell, I don't.
Why we are friends
Is a mystery to me.

BERT *is offended.*

QUEENIE (*weakly*): Very nice, dear.

BERT: It don't rhyme!

ADRIAN (*to* BERT): Would you mind if I sent your poem to the BBC, Bert?

BERT: Yes, I would. They're all a load of drug addicts in the BBC. I've got it on good authority.

QUEENIE (*impressed*): Oh, shocking! Know somebody high up, do you?

BERT: Yes — a window cleaner at Broadcasting House.
Everybody laughs. MATRON *enters.*

MATRON: Please! Your laughter is disturbing the other guests! Come along. (*She claps her hands.*) It's way past your bed time.

PANDORA: *Au contraire*, Matron! We can choose our own bed times.

MATRON: I was addressing myself to the oldsters, you cheeky young madam.
ADRIAN *and* PANDORA *leave.*

PANDORA:
ADRIAN: } Bye, Bert. Bye, Queenie!

BERT:
QUEENIE: } Bye!

MATRON: Time for bed.

BERT: Bed? It's still light — I'm used to staying up till after the Epilogue.

MATRON: Here, we go to bed at half past nine.

QUEENIE: We?
She looks coquettishly at BERT. BERT *laughs dirtily.*
QUEENIE *pushes* BERT *off.*

The Mole house. GEORGE *is in the hall banging the telephone.*

GEORGE: Bloody British Telecom! Come on, get your act together! Give me a dialling tone. (*He is getting increasingly enraged trying to get a line. Calling up to* ADRIAN:) Was there a storm in the night? Is the telephone pole still up?

ADRIAN (*calling down*): Oh no! Dad, I've got something to tell you!

GEORGE (*to* ADRIAN): Don't bother me now! (*To the phone:*) Come on. Come on! I want a job. I want some money in my pocket. I want to buy a round in the pub.

ADRIAN (*appearing with the phone bill*): Dad, we haven't paid the bill!

GEORGE: Because we haveb't *had* the bill, you daft pillock!

ADRIAN: But *I* have Dad. I put it under my mattress.

GEORGE: Have you gone barmy? The bills go behind the clock. (*Pause.*) *When* did you put it under your mattress?

ADRIAN: Two months ago, Dad. We're not on the phone any more!

GEORGE *grabs the bill and reads it.*

GEORGE (*stunned*): Two hundred and eighty seven pounds, thirty seven pence! (*Amazed:*) Operator calls: two hundred and thirty one pounds! (*Shouting:*) Who've you been phoning? The man in the bloody moon?

ADRIAN: No, Tunisia. Sorry Dad.

GEORGE (*weakly*): Sorry. He says he's sorry! He cuts me off from civilisation and he says he's sorry! I don't know why you don't finish me off completely, Adrian. Put rat poison in me tea. Come home one day and tell me you're pregnant. I give up. That's it. George Mole is no more. What you see is an empty shell.

GEORGE *goes out through the kitchen. The dog barks off.*

(*Off:*) Not you an' all!

ADRIAN *opens a telegram.*

ADRIAN: A telegram! Addressed to me! The BBC? No – from my mother. 'ADRIAN STOP COMING HOME STOP.' What does she mean? 'Stop coming home'? How can I stop coming home? I live here!

ADRIAN *goes into the house and up to his room to write his diary.* PAULINE *enters on the side of the stage. She is carrying her suitcases.*

Coming Down To Earth Again

PAULINE (*sings*): Coming down to earth again
Out of sunshine into twilight:
Coming down to earth again
From my rocket flight.

Coming down to earth again
Terra Firma out of the sky:
Coming round on earth again –
Touch-down from on high.

I've had my fling: I let my hair right down,
I dreamed that I could survive without ties:
Dreaming was fine but now it's wake-up time
And I'm rubbing the sleep from my eyes.

Hello the life I thought I'd shed for good
And hello people I'd blocked from my mind:
After the wine at last it's own-up time
In the world I left behind.

Coming down to earth again,
I'm back home − coming in − coming home . . .

PAULINE *goes upstairs and into the bedroom; she and*
GEORGE *kiss and hug.*

GEORGE: Adrian! Your mother's home!
ADRIAN *comes out of his room.*
Put the kettle on. We'll be down in a bit.
ADRIAN *comes downstairs and speaks to the audience.*

ADRIAN: My mother threw herself on the mercy of my father.
My father threw himself on the body of my mother. They've
been in bed for two days − on and off. My mother told me
why she left Rat-Fink Lucas. She said: 'Bimbo treated me like
a sex-object, Adrian, and he expected his evening meal cooked
for him, and he cut his toe-nails in the living-room! And,
besides, I'm very fond of your father . . .' She didn't mention
me! My only hope for future happiness now rests with the
BBC. If they would give me my own poetry programme on
Radio Four I would have an outlet for the intellectual side of
my nature. I haven't got enough emotions to cope with the
complexities of my everyday life. I rang Pandora and told her
that my mother had come back and she came round after her
viola lesson. I'm glad I've got her. Love is the only thing that
keeps me sane. Goodnight.
This is the end of the play, although the curtain call is done at
BERT *and* QUEENIE's *wedding. The cast wear their best*
clothes and flowers in their buttonholes. When BERT *and*
QUEENIE *take their call they are showered with confetti and*
rice. MR LUCAS *prepares to take the wedding photograph*
ADRIAN *enters last − just in time to be in the photograph.*

Music for the Play

Overture: The Mole Theme

The Mole Theme

This forms a part of the overture
and is also used between a number of scenes,
in varying musical styles, throughout the show
and as a background to the house-cleaning scene (page 29),
starting slowly and getting faster.

The House Where I Live

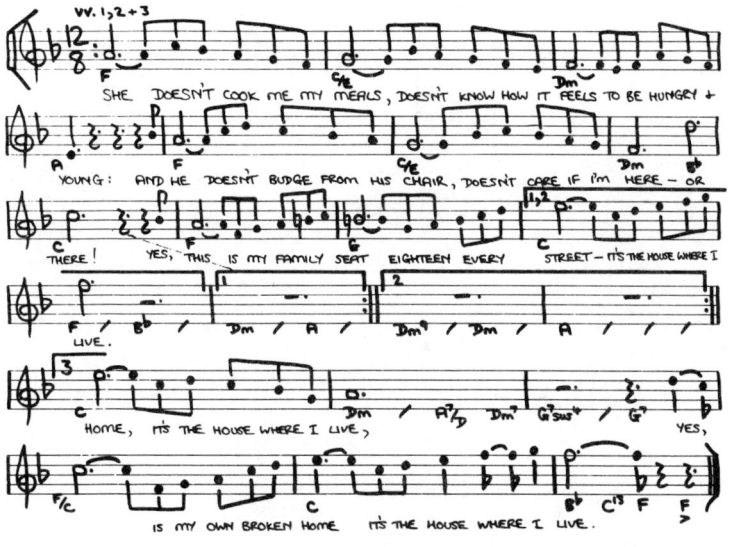

Sorry, Gotta Do It

The Bad Old Days

WHEN I WAS JUST A LAD, THINGS WERE FAR DIFFERENT THEN I CAN TELL YOU, MY FRIEND — THEY WERE TEN TIMES AS BAD! HAD ME NO GILDED YOUTH, BOY, LIT BY NO SUNSHINE RAYS — WE WERE FOURTEEN IN A HOVEL, TAKIN' LESSONS HOW TO GROVEL, IN THE BAD OLD DAYS. WE TOILED OUR YOUTH AWAY, BOY — NO MONEY, NO THANKS, NO PRAISE: THEY SAY "WHERE THERE'S MUCK THERE'S BRASS" — I SAY "NOT ON YOUR BLEEDIN' ARSE!" THEY WERE BAD OLD DAYS.

Your Hair of Gold

YOUR HAIR OF GOLD, YOUR EYES OF BABY BLUE — HOW COULD I EVER FACE A LIFE WITHOUT YOU? YOUR LIPS SO SWEET, YOUR TOUCH SO TENDER — YOU KNOW I SURRENDER TO EVERYTHING THAT YOU YOUR HEART.

Family Trio

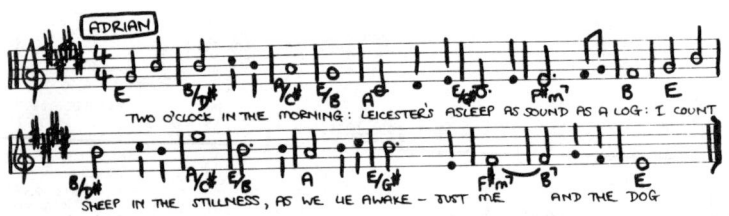

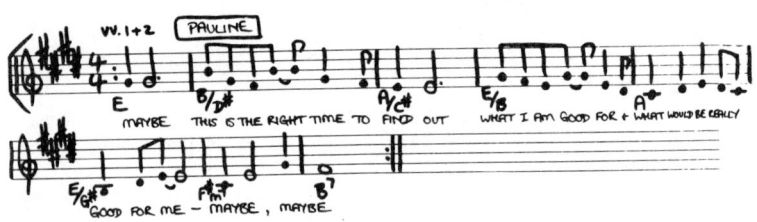

Your Dead Grandad

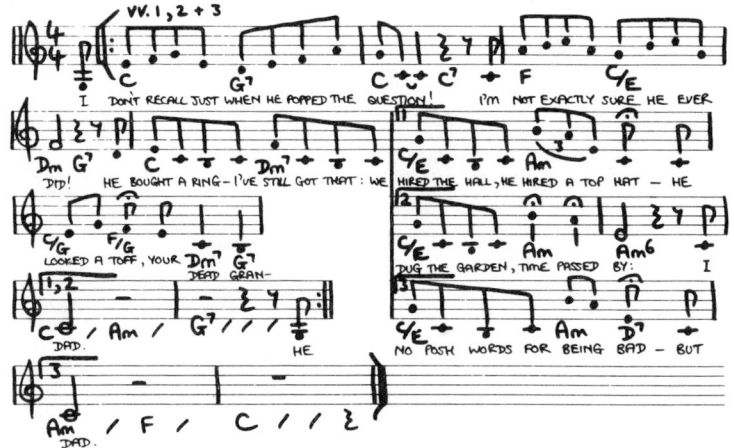

Get It Right!

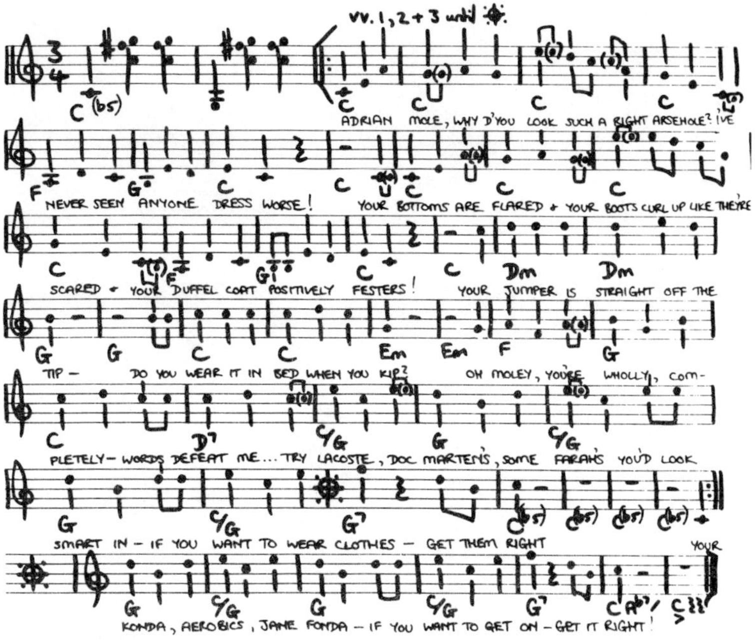

Dog

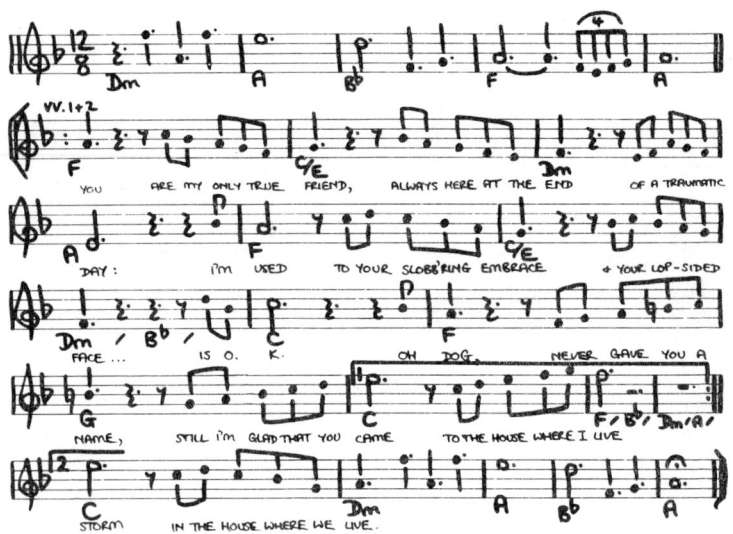

The Other Woman

Oh, Pandora

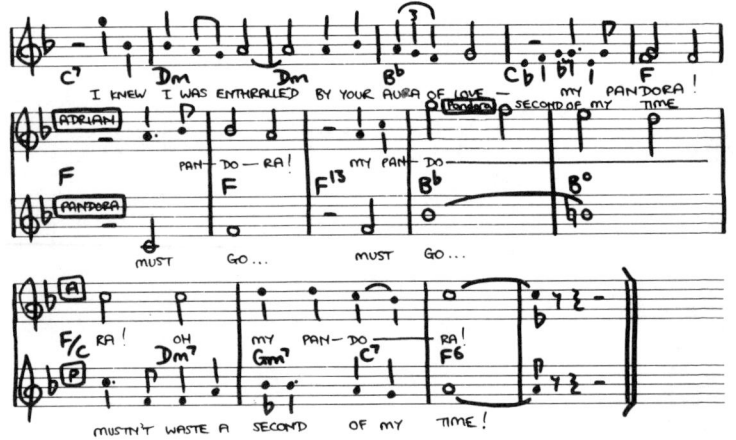

The Young Girl Inside You

Coming Down to Earth Again